I0814787

~ THE SOUTHERN FOOD & BEVERAGE MUSEUM ~

SoFAB COOK BOOK

THE SOUTHERN TABLE
Cynthia LeJeune Nobles, Series Editor

~ THE SOUTHERN FOOD & BEVERAGE MUSEUM ~

SoFAB COOK BOOK

RECIPES FROM THE MODERN SOUTH

ELIZABETH M. WILLIAMS & MADDIE HAYES

FOREWORD BY DICKIE BRENNAN

LOUISIANA STATE UNIVERSITY PRESS ~ BATON ROUGE

Published with the assistance of the V. Ray Cardozier Fund

Published by Louisiana State University Press
lsupress.org

Manufactured in Canada
First printing

DESIGNER: Michelle A. Neustrom
TYPEFACES: Source Serif Variable and Gotham, text; Lulo Clean, display
PRINTER AND BINDER: Friesens Corporation

Cover photographs: Watermelon Lemonade, Fried Chicken, Tomato Pie, and Low and Slow Spicy Brisket courtesy Maddie Hayes. Lox'd and Loaded courtesy Buffalo & Bergen. Bananas Foster courtesy Brennan's Restaurant.

Unless otherwise noted, all museum photographs appear courtesy of the Southern Food & Beverage Museum and all food photographs appear courtesy of Maddie Hayes.

LIBRARY OF CONGRESS CATALOGING-IN-PUBLICATION DATA

Names: Williams, Elizabeth M. (Elizabeth Marie), 1950–, author. | Hayes, Maddie, author. | Brennan, Dickie, writer of foreword.

Title: The Southern Food & Beverage Museum cookbook : recipes from the modern American south / Elizabeth M. Williams with Maddie Hayes ; foreword by Dickie Brennan.

Other titles: Southern Food and Beverage Museum cookbook

Description: Baton Rouge : Louisiana State University Press, [2024] | Series: The southern table | Includes index.

Identifiers: LCCN 2023045547 | ISBN 978-0-8071-8158-4 (cloth)

Subjects: LCSH: Cooking, American—Southern style. | Cooking—Southern States. | Southern Food and Beverage Museum | LCGFT: Cookbooks.

Classification: LCC TX715.2.S68 W542 2024 | DDC 641.5975—dc23/eng/20240212

LC record available at https://lccn.loc.gov/2023045547

To all the supporters of the
Southern Food & Beverage Museum (SoFAB),
especially those who did not think that
a food museum was a crazy idea.

You know who you are!

CONTENTS

FOREWORD

I COME FROM A FAMILY whose name is synonymous with New Orleans hospitality and cuisine, and my passion for cooking has been an intrinsic part of me for as long as I can remember. Through several apprenticeships, including with Chef Paul Prudhomme at Commander's Palace and Chef Larry Forgione at An American Place in New York City, as well as staging at Delmonico's in Mexico City and La Tour d'Argent in Paris, I cultivated a broad knowledge of cooking and of recipes, learning their origins and deep-rooted histories.

In 2008, I had the honor of being named chair of the Southern Food & Beverage Museum (SoFAB). My journey with SoFAB, however, started years earlier, when I had the pleasure of meeting its founder, Liz Williams. Liz had a vision of creating a place where culture and food intersect and could be studied. For almost twenty years, Liz has immersed herself in all things food and beverage. In her quest to see her vision become a reality, she reached out to chefs who were experts in the cuisine in their region. In this book, she shares the knowledge of these chefs with you.

As a chef and restaurateur operating six unique restaurants in the New Orleans area, I work with our chefs to identify dishes that will complement each restaurant's identity and heritage. Similarly, the recipes compiled in this book represent the best of southern cooking. For centuries, food has been the focal point of life. In the South especially, whether we are dining out or cooking at home with friends and family, most communal gatherings—from joyful celebrations to reverent commemorations—revolve around food. I hope these recipes help bring you and your family and friends together to experience the joy of raising a glass and sharing a meal. Cheers!

Dickie Brennan
New Orleans, Louisiana

~ THE SOUTHERN FOOD & BEVERAGE MUSEUM ~

SoFAB COOK BOOK

The Yellowhammer State
18 19
ALABAMA

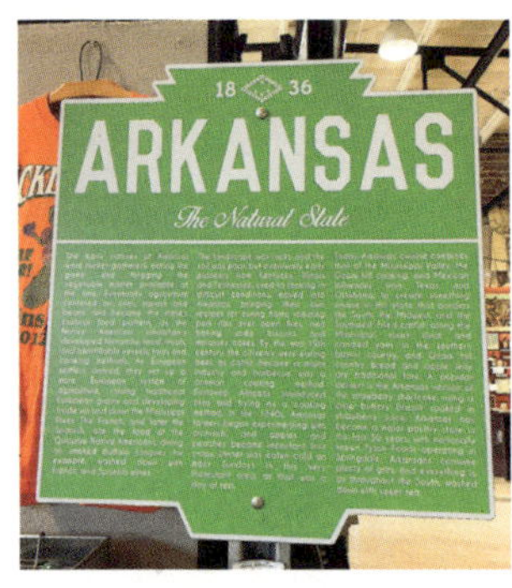
18 36
ARKANSAS
The Natural State

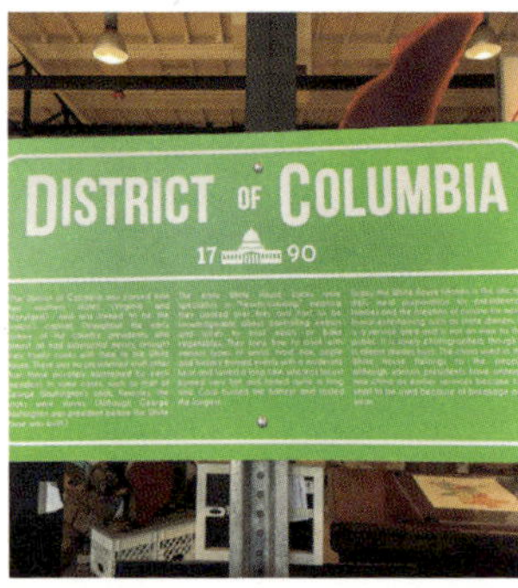
DISTRICT OF COLUMBIA
17 90

The Sunshine State
18 45
FLORIDA

The Peach State
17 88
GEORGIA

17 92
KENTUCKY
The Bluegrass State

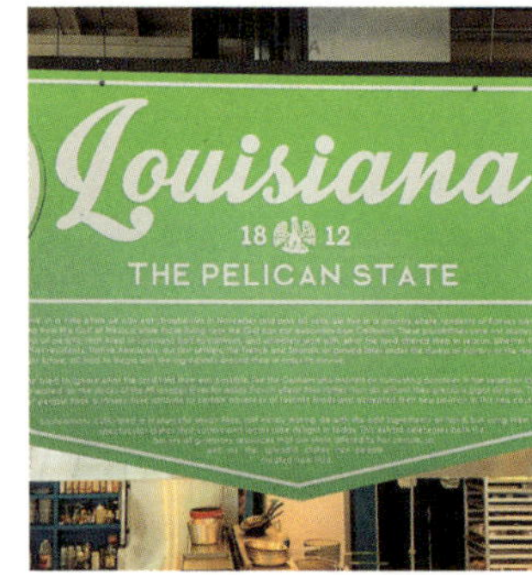
Louisiana
18 12
THE PELICAN STATE

17 88
MARYLAND
The Free State

MISSISSIPPI
The Magnolia State
1817

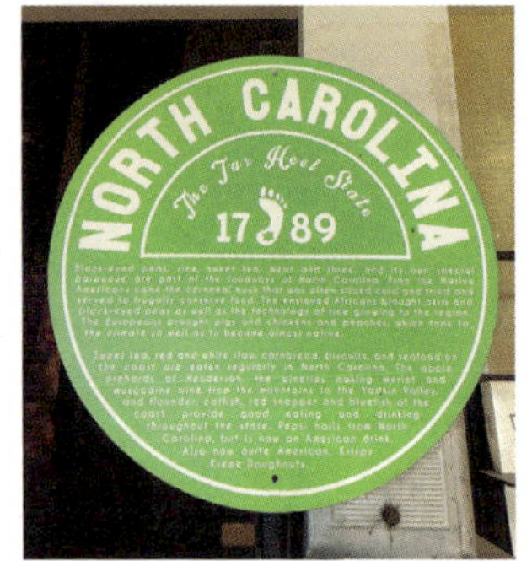
NORTH CAROLINA
The Tar Heel State
17 89

19 07
OKLAHOMA
The Sooner State

SOUTH CAROLINA
The Palmetto State
17 88

17 96
TENNESSEE
The Volunteer State

TEXAS
18 45
The Lone Star State

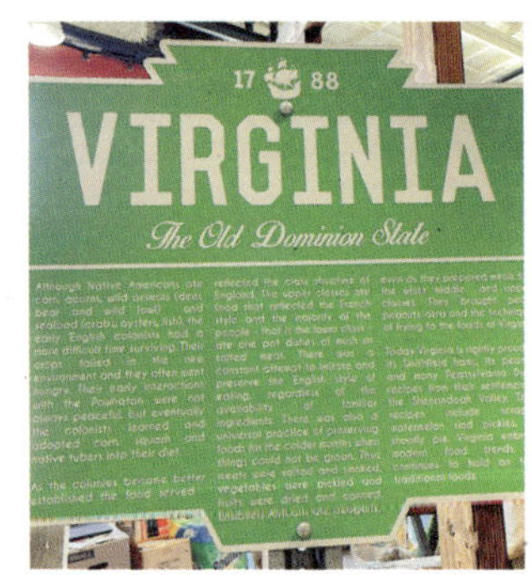
17 88
VIRGINIA
The Old Dominion State

WEST VIRGINIA
The Mountain State
1863

COOKING UP A FOOD MUSEUM

~ THE STORY OF SoFAB ~

ELIZABETH M. WILLIAMS

THE SOUTHERN FOOD & BEVERAGE MUSEUM began in 2003 as a humble idea hatched around a kitchen table. Since New Orleans is such a vibrant food city, the organizers found it remarkable that there was no museum that celebrated our rich culinary heritage. In fact, when we opened the museum in 2008, New Orleans's reputation as a food mecca was so pervasive that people outside the city were also surprised that one didn't already exist. Hence, our reception was overwhelmingly positive.

Unlike art museums, which nearly every large city seems to boast, food and drink museums are few and far between. Early in the twenty-first century, the United States had a handful of inspired food destinations, such as San Francisco, Charleston, New York, and Chicago, in addition to New Orleans; each had its own style and claim to fame. Food obsession has since certainly spread outside the Crescent City to encompass the whole country (or even much of the world), but that was not the case in 2003.

SoFAB began in one of those Judy Garland/Mickey Rooney-like scenes of a group of people having a spirited "wouldn't it be great if" conversation. Then either Judy or Mickey would say, "Well, let's do it! Let's put on a show!" and the entire group would agree. The rest of the movie would be dedicated to organizing and finally putting on a show—except in our case, it was a museum. And we really did it, instead of just pretending to do so. At some point in our early conversations, wine and cocktails also may have been involved.

By 2004 we had established a nonprofit, tax-exempt corporation and were looking for a suitable location to house the museum. At the same time, we were creating our concept, a website, logo, and ideas for programming and fundraising. The very first, lean-and-mean board was made up of myself as president, Matt Konigsmark, and Gina

Warner. Dana Honn built and designed our first website. Graphic designer Monique McCall designed our logo, which is still in use today; it hangs over our door, announcing us to the street. Virginia Miller helped us promote the idea. Around Virginia's table at the Beuerman Miller marketing firm, we came up with the acronym SoFAB, which has served us well.

While we were fundraising, we learned that no one had a clue about what a food museum might actually be, so we decided to create pop-up exhibits to illustrate our concept. (Note: No one called these things "pop-ups" in those days. We called them "temporary exhibits in borrowed space," certainly sounding less avant-garde but successful nonetheless.)

We were busy creating infrastructure, fundraising, proselytizing, and making connections, and we needed help designing our first exhibit. That person who "helped," based on a casual conversation on the sidewalk after a chance encounter, turned out to be the inimitable drinks historian Elizabeth Pearce. She created "Toast of New Orleans," an exhibit that opened in a space at the New Orleans Centre, a mall near the Superdome that housed a branch of Saks Fifth Avenue. That area is now called Champions Square. Elizabeth was marvelously creative, telling the story of the famous drinks of New Orleans—from nectar soda and coffee with chicory to the Sazerac and Ramos Gin Fizz—with no more than smoke and mirrors and aplomb. (Elizabeth has a theater background, so she was familiar with smoke and mirrors.) Our New Orleans drink exhibit was staffed by an intern. It was also written up in *USA Today*. We had begun.

The look of the museum was created by graphic designer Megan Pendergrass. She helped us pick colors and created business cards, whose design we still use today. She created the museum's text panels and designed the website. She also selected typeface fonts, all of which helped us establish a public identity and carried us forward until our move to our new building on Oretha Castle Haley Boulevard.

Our small but powerful—and extremely talented—group of volunteers made our upstart museum look like it was old and established. Then we mounted a second pop-up (accompanied by a grand party) throughout the public spaces of the Riverwalk Marketplace. SoFAB's exhibit opened in January 2005 but was shut down a few months later by Hurricane Katrina in August. The city was devastated. The exhibit in the mall—fortunately mounted without artifacts—was lost. "Tout de Suite—All about Sugar" seemed an apt name for an exhibit that wasn't available for viewing very long. (We later reused the name for a comprehensive exhibit about sugar that we mounted in our first permanent location.)

During this trying time, all of us who were working fanatically on this unusual passion project had other compelling things to attend to. Like the city, we began to rebuild.

By 2008 we were ready to take a chance again on a food and beverage museum, and we thought that the city was ready too. A fear of hurricanes, however, made tourists and conventions slow to return. At the time, the Riverwalk was never full. A once-bustling linear mall along the Mississippi River, which had housed some high-end shops, was just limping along awaiting the full return of tourism. After some deliberation, mall management allowed us to take over a space that had been a dress shop at the end of the mall near the Morial Convention Center and the food court. They gave us a kinfolk deal, and we were off.

Dickie Brennan, New Orleans chef and restaurateur, was chair when we reopened in 2008. Once again Elizabeth Pearce came through as a curator. We hired a design/build contractor to convert the retail clothing store into a museum and formally opened in July 2008. Our ribbon-cutting ceremony featured two native Louisianans: the commissioner of the Department of Agriculture and Forestry, Mike Strain, DVM, and Rear Admiral Stephen Rochon. Admiral Rochon was then the director of the Executive Residence and the White House chief usher. The admiral lent us the chef's jacket of White House executive chef Cristeta Comerford and brought with him executive pastry chef Bill Yosses. We were on our way once more.

We continued to improve our exhibits, augment our programming, and learn what we needed to do to be a truly sustainable business. Since those fledgling days, the organization has flourished and expanded, always trying to remain true to its mission of documenting the food and drink culture of the American South, as well as educating the public about it. Our stay at the Riverwalk was our incubation period.

In 2014, we moved into our own building on Oretha Castle Haley Boulevard, with hundreds of people attending the reopening ceremony. We were fortunate enough to call once again on Commissioner Strain. We also invited Lt. Governor Jay Dardenne to talk about the importance of food and cuisine not only as part of Louisiana's aesthetic identity but also economically and culturally.

Over time, we expanded our board to include chefs who saw merit in the idea of a food museum. Our museum houses a continually improving and rapidly growing collection that reflects the states in America's southeastern quadrant, with a temporary gallery for rotating exhibits, a demonstration kitchen, a professional kitchen, and a food lab. We chose to use the post–World War II New South as our geographic boundaries without cutting any states in half.

SoFAB has won awards for preservation because of its activities as a conservator of artifacts of the kitchen and dining room and for educating the public about the past through food. The museum has won additional recognition for its restoration of our current building, the old Dryades Market.

The exterior of the Southern Food & Beverage Museum.

OUR LARGEST ARTIFACT

We moved into our largest artifact, the old Dryades Market, in 2014. In its heyday, New Orleans had an established market system, boasting more than thirty markets, one in each new neighborhood as it was established. The Dryades Market began in 1849 as an open-air covered market in the Faubourg Lafayette. (A faubourg is a neighborhood.) It was located on what was once Dryades Street. In 1912, flagging sales forced the city to tear down the aging pavilion. On the same spot, the city—in the hopes that a structure with walls would revive the market's popularity—built the enclosed market building that we now occupy. During World War II, the building was used as a motor pool. Shortly after the war, the City of New Orleans sold it. In 1989, the street name "Dryades" was changed to Oretha Castle Haley Boulevard, in honor of a beloved civil rights activist who lived in the neighborhood. The renovation of the building as a museum was designed by architect Jonathan Tate and constructed by Woodward Design + Build. Their work received a historic preservation award from the Louisiana Landmarks Society.

Our building still reveals its history. The floor demarcates the original market stalls in blackish-green terrazzo borders. Orange terrazzo marks the aisles. The original cement floors of the stalls are still visible. There's an interesting system of trusses in the ceiling. We left that exposed, which allows you to see the structure that supports the roof span and makes it possible for the building to be so open.

We use the entire space, hanging objects and signs from the lofty ceiling. We have hung boats, old signs, and even a large golden king-cake baby. Those hanging artifacts make the space feel comfortably full instead of vast and empty.

We installed our demonstration kitchen in the former fish market section of the building. This space opens out onto a garden and outdoor cooking space that we call the Gumbo Garden, which holds large artifacts, outdoor cooking equipment, a covered area, and boxed raised beds filled with specimen plants. Attached stairs allow children to peek into the beds. The Gumbo Garden is a great party space as well.

Because our building is a former market, we treat each state's permanent exhibit as a market stall, thereby compartmentalizing our exhibit space, "The Gallery of the South—States of Taste." It is through these displays of artifacts that we tell the dynamic story of southern food and drink. The artifacts are arranged together as a market stall would be, instead of being separately exhibited as objects. When the same foods, like corn, are found throughout the South, we aim to show how they are used differently in each state. That is why we developed trails, which are themed walks throughout the museum. As we continue to create a deeper, more nuanced experience in SoFAB, more trails will emerge.

A glimpse of some of the hanging artifacts in the Southern Food & Beverage Museum.

Our most highly developed trail is that of Smoke and Fire. Processes like cooking over coals low and slow, smoking to cure meats like ham and sausage, smoking to add flavor to fish, and grilling to pop open oysters more easily are so prevalent in the South that SoFAB decided not to have a specific exhibit about barbecue. With the support of noted TV host and barbecue expert Steven Raichlen as our barbecue curator, we instead addressed barbecue within each state's exhibit. That became our trail of Smoke and Fire.

It is incredibly exciting to return the building back to the service of food, obviously not as a market but as a food and drink museum. Visitors can see how the states' food cultures are the same but different, and so can you through chapters devoted to each southern state in this book.

MIXING DRINKS: THE MUSEUM OF THE AMERICAN COCKTAIL AND LA GALERIE DE L'ABSINTHE

We southerners are known for our drinking. The stereotype of the bootlegger is even centered in the hills of the South, where "entrepreneurs" distilled whiskey despite a national prohibition of making and selling the stuff. Therefore, the Southern Food & Beverage Museum is a fine and appropriate home for MOTAC, the Museum of the American Cocktail.

MOTAC was founded by celebrity bartender Dale DeGroff and a handful of others who were part of the craft cocktail movement. Its artifacts tell the story of the development of the cocktail, beginning with the invention of distillation, to the early nineteenth-century widespread acceptance of the word "cocktail" (from the early Cock Tail), to tiki bars that emerged in the mid-twentieth century, and to the craft cocktail movement that is still blessedly with us. The modern cocktail movement is still evolving, so we will be adding artifacts for the modern era bit by bit. We cannot get ahead of history, but it is a pleasant problem to have.

MOTAC installed its first exhibit in New Orleans at the Pharmacy Museum in the French Quarter. Fortunately, the exhibit and its artifacts were unharmed by Hurricane

A wall in the Museum of the American Cocktail.

Katrina. The exhibit was boxed up, and in 2006 it reopened at the Aladdin Casino in Las Vegas in the Commander's Palace Restaurant. The casino was eventually sold, and Commander's in Las Vegas closed. When SoFAB moved to its new location, it merged with MOTAC, and the two are now comfortably housed together.

An important part of MOTAC is La Galerie de l'Absinthe. Absinthe is a strong anise-flavored, green-colored spirit that, in the late 1800s, was blamed for causing hallucinations. Before it was banned in 1912 in the United States, New Orleans was the absinthe drinking capital of America. Our gallery reflects the culture of drinking absinthe by evoking the Old Absinthe House on Bourbon Street in New Orleans circa 1895. This exhibit, which is the biggest display of absinthe artifacts in the country, is largely the result of the collecting fervor of local historian Ray Bordelon, as well as his design skills. Not only does it showcase the beginnings of absinthe, but it also outlines the rituals of drinking it, the obsessions of the demimonde (those on the moral fringes), and the way New Orleans took to the "green fairy." Absinthe looms large in the cocktails of the city, the lore of the city, and even in the city's beloved absinthe substitute, Herbsaint.

A fun aspect of both SoFAB and MOTAC is the ability to enjoy a cocktail while visiting the museum and viewing the exhibits. Drinking is not limited to certain areas of the museum. We recommend that you get something to drink while you walk around, whether it is a drink that is soft or hard. It makes the experience more fun.

Hard and soft drinks can be purchased at the bar from SoFAB's Bruning's Restaurant, one of the museum's very special artifacts. There once was a restaurant and bar built on stilts over Lake Pontchartrain in the West End, a shoreline area then on the outskirts of the city that was a park and amusement space. The third oldest restaurant in the city, it was founded by Theodor Bruning, a German immigrant. Over the decades the restaurant survived many hurricanes. In 1998, Hurricane Georges struck the final blow to the original building, rendering it unsafe. Years earlier, the family had the foresight to purchase a two-story building at the water's edge at the base of the boardwalk that had been the original path leading up to Bruning's. After Hurricane Georges, the family moved the bar and restaurant to the new building. But the famous mahogany Brunswick bar, built from a kit, was too tall for the new space. It was placed in storage.

In 2005, Hurricane Katrina hit New Orleans like a ton of bricks, and the storm surge took out Bruning's new building. Rising water flooded the restaurant's storage facility and the bar. It remained submerged until the city pumped out the standing water. While the building was inundated by water, the glue holding the bar together dissolved, and the bar's finish was compromised. Eventually the family donated the bar to SoFAB, and we put its 176 pieces back together. Many a loving volunteer helped us restore the finish.

EDUCATION AT SOFAB

The SoFAB Research Center and the John and Bonnie Boyd Hospitality and Culinary Library at Nunez Community College together offer a research library and archive dedicated to collecting cookbooks, menus, and other literature related to the study and practice of the culinary arts. It is located on Nunez's campus, headquartered in the town of Chalmette in St. Bernard Parish, just south of New Orleans. SoFAB curates a food-related exhibit at the Research Center.

The John and Bonnie Boyd Hospitality and Culinary Library opened at Nunez Community College in 2013 and grew in size and depth into the SoFAB Research Center, which opened in the fall of 2022. The center contains more than forty thousand culinary books, as well as food and cocktail menus, pamphlets, archival documents, and a growing number of important collections and ephemera, all gathered by and donated to the Southern Food & Beverage Museum. It houses the papers of chefs such as Louis Osteen and writers like Mildred Covert, as well as the book collections and ephemera of Bonnie Tandy Leblang, Poppy Tooker, Norman Van Aken, Paul Prudhomme, Mildred Covert, Frank Davis, Ken Smith, and others. It is also a depository for books contributed by members of Les Dames d'Escoffier International.

The SoFAB Research Center serves as a unique resource for residents, visitors, scholars, and researchers from various fields, including history, culture, fitness, nu-

Breaking bread at the opening of the SoFAB Culinary Research Center at Nunez Community College.

trition, policy, public health, and more. A growing number of books are printed in languages other than English.

National Culinary Heritage Register

SoFAB created and maintains the National Culinary Heritage Register, an expansive list of culinary products, processes, inventions, traditions, and establishments that are at least fifty years old and have contributed significantly to the development of American foodways. The first and only register of its kind, the National Culinary Heritage Register explores and preserves the complex history of food and beverages in America. The Register is a treasure trove of information for researchers and includes (1) enterprises that may be associated with a specific building or property, such as continuously operating restaurants, stores, factories, mills, farms, and distilleries; (2) subjects, such as culinary inventions, processes, and traditions that may be attached to a geographical location, like a city or region, but not a specific physical site; and (3) establishments like restaurants, stores, and factories that no longer exist but were of particular historical significance to America's food and beverage culture. Information about becoming a part of the Register can be found on our website.

The Paul C. P. McIlhenny Culinary Entrepreneurship Program

The Paul C. P. McIlhenny Culinary Entrepreneurship Program, established by SoFAB and supported by the McIlhenny Family Foundation, is designed to encourage food start-up businesses in the area, to offer real-world educational business training for aspiring chefs and other culinary professionals, and to provide direct field and work experience for students studying for a career in the food and beverage industry. The program partners and cooperates with other entrepreneurial programs to avoid duplication and provide depth of service. The following examples show how it strives to promote growth, learning, and opportunity among its target populations.

FOR BUSINESS OWNERS AND CULINARY PROFESSIONALS

Master classes are conducted at the Southern Food & Beverage Museum by established chefs for aspiring chefs in New Orleans. Quarterly informational programs are offered for culinary entrepreneurs and start-up food business owners. In addition, depending on the type of product that the entrepreneur has in mind, there is the potential for sales in the museum gift shop.

Those opening restaurants and bars may host cooking and drink demonstrations or pop-up dinners at the museum. As much as possible, SoFAB offers assistance with marketing by featuring businesses in the museum newsletter, informing journalists about the program and the entrepreneurs, and using social media.

We lease out, on an hourly basis and at a below-market rate, SoFAB's certified commercial kitchens and Bruning's bar.

FOR STUDENTS

We help students by providing summer- and semester-long internships in various fields of study. We hold "Mentor Conversations" between food professionals and culinary students. Food professionals include not only chefs but also food journalists, photographers, executives in manufacturing and processing facilities, and other professionals working in the food and beverage industry.

NITTY GRITS NETWORK

Nitty Grits is a dynamic network of producers, hosts, and authors whose work examines food and drink in all its diversity across the United States and the world. It produces and distributes a curated slate of audio and video podcasts, web series, and other filmed entertainment, as well as publishing projects. Offerings focus on a broad spectrum of culinary subjects and a comprehensive array of issues—from cooking, drinking, and eating to food policy, agricultural sustainability, and waste management.

CLASSES FOR ENTHUSIASTS

SoFAB offers all manner of classes for enthusiasts, from how to sharpen knives and keep your cast- iron pans in good order to Cajun and Creole cooking classes. Chef Dee Lavigne, SoFAB's director of culinary programming, offers an in-depth look into how to create delicious, traditional dishes that can be found nowhere else in the world, while discussing their cultural and historical origins. Some classes are demonstrations, and others are truly hands-on. Some are private, and some are open to everyone. In every case, there is a large dose of culture, heritage, and history.

~ ~ ~

SoFAB is still one of the United States' few independent food museums, one not associated with a brand or category of food. In 2018, we celebrated ten years of operation. Six years later, we look back at our many accomplishments. And since we began our pop-ups in 2004, we consider 2024 our twentieth anniversary year.

We are especially thankful that we were spared from the five hurricanes that made landfall in Louisiana in 2020. We do, however, continue to weather the COVID pandemic, which hit the New Orleans food, beverage, and cultural worlds particularly hard. Thankfully, tourism is gradually increasing, and the restaurant industry is improving. We invite everyone, whether local or just passing through our great city, to come visit SoFAB. We couldn't be prouder of this amazing organization and all that we have accomplished over the last thirteen years.

TELLING STORIES: WHAT YOU'LL FIND IN THIS BOOK

One of the countless lessons I learned while opening SoFAB is that the most impactful way to reach people is to tell a good story. And we southerners are known for our stories.

In 2008, while New Orleans was recovering from the devastation that followed Hurricane Katrina, a small motley group of dedicated dreamers opened SoFAB in the Riverwalk Marketplace, a shopping mall situated along the Mississippi River. Early on we decided that we would not be a museum that is afraid of food and drink. And so, we have always allowed people to eat and drink (including alcoholic beverages) in the museum. Imagine being tantalized by stories about food and not being able to eat it? And because we consider the exhibits in the museum to be approachable, we invite visitors to touch many artifacts. We know from our own lives that eating is not a rarified experience, nor should visiting a museum.

From the beginning, tourists and New Orleans residents came to see what we had to say about southern food. Visitors were naturally curious, but they were also looking for tastes, recipes, and a place to read and hear southern stories. Because we were initially short on artifacts, a lot of our exhibits were merely words and recipes on placards placed around the walls and on tables and shelves. Despite our sparse exhibits, opening the museum must have filled a need that we did not know was there.

We quickly learned that people have spirited opinions about what belongs in a food and drink museum. Much to our delight, those early visitors all had their own stories as well. After viewing the exhibits, they would often linger, eager to share with us interesting and entertaining tales so often filled with memories of family and friends. Soon, people were donating artifacts and ephemera. Those artifacts have helped us build more thoughtful and comprehensive exhibits and to expand the stories that we tell and the voices that we include. Almost everything in our collections has been donated.

One thing we have learned on our museum journey is that the answer to the question "What is southern food?" is one that reflects the dynamism of the South. The foundation of southern food begins with the Native People and their food, with the foods and expectations of Europe, and, importantly, the labor and flavors of Africa built on that base. Each group of immigrants who made their way to the South, whether they settled in many states or in just small pockets, has made its culinary mark.

A beer event at SoFAB with the Brewseum in Chicago, the Urban South Brewery in New Orleans, and Illuminated Brew Works, Chicago.

We define southern food as food that is eaten in the South, whether it is chicken masala or tamales or gumbo. Cuisine is a social invention, and much of what has developed relies on the bounties of the fields and the waters, the spices of the world that have traveled to the South, and the agricultural, cooking, and preserving techniques that are both Indigenous and borrowed. Other influences come from shared ideas and experiences. Since the beginning, southerners have used imagination and ingenuity to overcome the challenges of limited time and money, as well as scarce basic resources, such as utensils.

No matter their differences, southerners enjoy the pleasures of the table. It is important to note that, at its heart, southern food is really food that is prepared and eaten at home. Eating in a restaurant on a regular basis and considering the food there as representative of the region are very modern concepts. Today, with the harried pace of life and so many people eating out often, we can forget that cuisine began at home and not in restaurants. The trend of eating out has become even stronger today because most of us are busy, and the role of restaurants has changed in response. But despite our hectic lives, or perhaps because of them, we are looking for both the comfort of traditional food and the excitement of eating the new. We hope that this cookbook satisfies both these itches.

Southern food is always changing and evolving. That means it is not moribund but is a dynamic, ever-evolving cultural basis for well-being and identity. This book therefore contains recipes and histories of both traditional and contemporary southern foods. Almost every person who lives in the South, even if they are originally from the Pacific Northwest or New England, has a definition of what constitutes southern food. That list of ubiquitous foods could also include brand-name products such as Tabasco and Pepsi, and we touch on the stories of those foods here.

This book offers a view of the southern kitchen and table that is modern in its sensibilities but also respectful of the past. Some traditional dishes, for instance, may have a new twist. Many of our recipes come from creative chefs who have either stayed in the South, having been born here, or settled in the South because they found a home here. Although most recipes from chefs were developed for restaurants, the ones in this book are adapted for your home kitchen.

Other recipes are contributed by staff and friends of SoFAB. Some are traditional, and some are personal to the contributor. Some dishes come from home cooks who are so familiar with the recipes that they can seem cryptic and idiosyncratic, such as one from my grandmother, who used a particular broken teacup as a measuring cup.

We also try to communicate the entire story of the dish: how it should be served and when it is served, who might serve it, and what kind of china and serving pieces to use. Take the humble watermelon, for example. It can be eaten outdoors and form the basis of a seed-spitting contest or be pressed and salted for inclusion in a watermelon and tomato salad served on fine china with lump crabmeat. We also point out that some dishes are too time consuming or too expensive for the everyday table, but it would be horrible to imagine certain occasions without them. So those dishes are included too. You can appreciate that.

While we are at it, we take you on a journey through the South's many liquid refreshments. Whether it is the debate over sweet tea or unsweetened tea, chicory coffee or pure, moonshine or bourbon, there is serious drinking in the South. Selecting the right beverage is just as important as selecting the right food. We include recipes and stories about all sorts of southern drinks that are poured for lots of occasions.

We tried to select recipes that adhere to the idea that southern food is traditional, that apply southern techniques and cooking methods to new ingredients, or that incorporate the foods of various migrants to the South. We are not trying to write the quintessential southern cookbook—we are writing the SoFAB cookbook. You might not find your favorite southern dish, but we hope that you discover some new recipes that reflect the culture and warmth of southern food. We also hope that these recipes reflect the warmth and fun of SoFAB. All these dishes will feel and taste southern, and they will fit comfortably on your southern table.

Yes, the South is about stories. In this book you'll find lots of lore that, through the lens of food, gives a glimpse of the soul of the South. We expand these stories by using the resources of the museum, particularly through photos and artifacts that illustrate time and place. We hope this book becomes a staple on your counter. We hope that its pages become stained by food and drink from happy times cooking and eating. And we hope that it also finds a place on your bedside table for dreaming about meals to share.

The original facade, counter, and screen door of Big Bob Gibson Bar-B-Q, alongside other Alabama specialties.

ALABAMA

ALABAMA SITS ON THE GULF OF MEXICO but extends northward into the heart of the South. Its history is a rural one, and its people have known great poverty. As a result, much of this state's early cuisine was a response to scarcity.

After European colonization, Alabama's land was farmed by enslaved Africans, yielding staple crops such as peanuts, pecans, and corn, in addition to cotton. In the nineteenth century, the Port of Mobile brought in bananas, introducing tropical fruit to the state. Over the years, immigrants from Korea, Greece, Vietnam, India, China, France, Lebanon, and recently Mexico have added yet another layer of complexity to the flavors of Alabama.

The typical food of Alabama is simple, straightforward, and honest; not much has changed in its preparation. It revolves around native foods, such as corn, wild legumes, sweet potatoes, nuts, and game, as well as fresh Gulf seafood. Alabamans embrace dishes such as barbecue, chicken stew, and banana pudding. Mealtime staples also include biscuits, fried chicken, goat stew, and thin, crispy, pan-fried lacy cornbread. (And don't forget greens and any of the myriad of southern peas!) Like the whole Gulf region, Alabamans enjoy gumbo. Decadent and boozy Lane Cake is the state's signature dessert.

CHICKEN & DUMPLINGS

MADDIE HAYES | MAKES 6 SERVINGS

2 tablespoons butter
2 carrots, diced
2 stalks celery and their leaves, diced
1 onion, diced
3 cloves garlic, minced
¼ cup all-purpose flour
½ cup dry white wine
4 cups low-sodium chicken stock or broth
½ cup half-and-half or whole milk
1 bay leaf
1 teaspoon chopped fresh thyme
2 cups cooked, diced. or shredded chicken
Salt and freshly ground black pepper, to taste
¾ cup frozen peas
Unbaked Drop Biscuits dough (page 36) or canned biscuits
For serving: fresh parsley

Melt the butter in a large pot over medium high heat, and sauté the carrots, celery, and onion until softened and beginning to brown, about 3 minutes. Add the garlic and sauté 1 minute, stirring constantly. The garlic should be fragrant. Add the flour and stir to coat. Deglaze with white wine, making sure to scrape up all the fond—the brown bits—on the bottom of the pot.

Add chicken broth and bring to a boil. Turn the heat down to a simmer, and add the half-and-half, bay leaf, and thyme. Stir in the chicken and season with salt and pepper. Stir in the peas and bring to a simmer. Gently drop tablespoonful of biscuit dough into the simmering pot. (If you're using canned biscuits, cut each into fourths.)

Cover and simmer over low heat until dumplings are fluffy, cooked through, and float to the top, about 15 minutes. No peeking! Serve garnished with fresh parsley and freshly ground pepper.

LEGG'S CORNBREAD DRESSING

CHUCK PURVIS | MAKES 8–10 SERVINGS

In the South, when something is stuffed inside a bird or a vegetable, it is called "dressing." It's "stuffing" when it is cooked on the side.

A. C. Legg has been making seasonings since 1923. The company's sage-forward Dressing Seasoning uses the highest-quality sage. Easy to find at grocery stores and online, it has always been a favorite in our home.

3½ cups cornbread crumbs
3½ cups white breadcrumbs, slightly toasted
½ cup (1 stick) butter
1 cup finely chopped celery
1 cup finely chopped onion
2 cups turkey broth
½ cup milk
2 large eggs, slightly beaten
1 tablespoon Legg's Dressing Seasoning

Preheat the oven to 350°F. Grease the insides of a 9 × 13-inch baking pan and set aside.

In a large bowl, mix together the cornbread crumbs and white breadcrumbs. Set aside. Melt the butter in a skillet, and sauté the celery and the onion until soft, around 8 minutes. Add the vegetable mixture and any remaining butter to the bowl of crumbs. To the crumbs, add the turkey broth, milk, eggs, and Legg's Dressing Seasoning, and mix thoroughly. Place the mixture in the prepared pan and even out the top. Bake until brown, 25–35 minutes. Serve warm.

Photo courtesy of Camille Staub.

PICKLED SHRIMP SALAD WITH BUTTERMILK DRESSING

COLLEEN ALLERTON-HOLLIER & CAMILLE STAUB

MAKES 20 HORS D'OEUVRE SERVINGS

This recipe is a bit long on ingredients and takes some work, but it is worth the effort. This spectacular salad is delicious and looks beautiful on a platter at a party. There will be no leftovers.

PICKLED SHRIMP

1 gallon water
4 stalks celery, chopped
1 yellow onion, diced
1 fennel bulb, chopped
1 cup white wine
4 tablespoons salt
2 lemons, cut in half
2 limes, cut in half
2 oranges, cut in half
4 pounds large Gulf shrimp, heads on and unpeeled
Wooden skewers
1 quart rice vinegar
A large bowl of ice water

To pickle shrimp, add water, celery, onion, fennel, wine, and salt to a large pot. Bring to a boil, lower heat to a simmer, and cook 20 minutes to allow the flavors to meld. Add lemons, limes, and oranges, squeezing and dropping each half directly into the bouillon. Simmer an additional 10 to 20 minutes, depending on how strong you want the flavor. Strain and return liquid to the pot.

Skewer shrimp with wooden skewers to keep them straight while cooking; this will make them more uniform when cleaning and portioning. Poach the skewered shrimp in the liquid until just cooked through, 3–5 minutes. Check for doneness by removing the head. Meat should be just slightly translucent in the center.

Shock cooked shrimp in ice water and allow to fully chill, 5–10 minutes. Peel shrimp and marinate in rice vinegar 30 minutes, fully submerged.

Strain and save the rice vinegar. Devein and portion shrimp by cutting them in half lengthwise, removing the vein and slicing into thirds on a bias. Refrigerate until needed.

BUTTERMILK DRESSING

MAKES ABOUT 2 CUPS

1 pint buttermilk
1 cup grated Grana Padano or Parmesan cheese
½ cup mayonnaise
2 teaspoons Dijon mustard
2 cloves garlic
1 tablespoon red wine vinegar
1½ teaspoons Worcestershire sauce
½ teaspoon white pepper
1 teaspoon salt
1 anchovy
1 tablespoon lemon juice

Place all ingredients in a blender and puree until smooth. Adjust seasoning.

Assembly

1 pint Buttermilk Dressing
1 cup rye bread croutons, ¼-inch dice
Reserved cleaned shrimp
3 stalks celery, peeled and sliced ½ inch thick, any yellow celery leaves reserved
1 teaspoon celery seed salt
½ cup reserved rice vinegar
½ cup olive oil
3 ounces trout roe
2 avocados, 1-inch dice
2 radishes, shaved thin and soaked in ice water
1 fresh jalapeño pepper, shaved thin and soaked in ice water
2 tablespoons chili oil
Large flake sea salt

To complete the dish, evenly spread the buttermilk dressing on the bottom of your favorite serving platter or in individual serving bowls. Top with croutons.

In a large mixing bowl, add shrimp, celery, and celery seed. Season with salt. Taste and add vinegar, olive oil, and trout roe. Taste and adjust seasoning.

Place the dressed shrimp over the buttermilk and croutons. Be sure to remove all the roe out of any leftover liquid and spoon it over the top of the shrimp. Garnish with avocados, radishes, jalapeño, celery leaf, and flake salt. Drip the chili oil around the exposed rim of buttermilk dressing.

SMOKED FISH DIP

CAMILLE STAUB | MAKES 4 CUPS

1½ pounds smoked catfish, skin removed
½ cup sour cream
½ cup cream cheese, at room temperature
½ cup Duke's mayonnaise
Zest and juice of 1 lemon
2 tablespoons minced shallot
2 tablespoons chopped fresh dill
1 teaspoon ground black pepper
1 teaspoon salt
¼ teaspoon chili pepper flakes
For serving: toast points, saltine crackers, or chips

Using a mixer with a whisk attachment, combine all ingredients in a large bowl and mix on medium speed until mixture is smooth and there are no large pieces of smoked fish left, about 2 minutes. Serve with toast points, saltines, or chips.

TOMATO PIE

BRENT ROSEN | MAKES 1 (9-INCH) PIE

Although the tomato is technically a fruit, we southerners consider it one of our great vegetables. This savory pie takes full advantage of these flavorful summer treats. Typically, a tomato pie would call for non-heirloom tomatoes because heirlooms tend to be juicer, and when those juices are released, you get a soggy pie. To avoid that problem, our recipe recommends roasting the tomatoes before putting them into the pie crust. The roasting will not only dry the tomatoes but caramelize them, adding an additional layer of flavor. Our pie features fresh herbs, tart shallots, and extra-sharp white cheddar cheese, so that the flavors surrounding your heirloom tomatoes are equal to them in deliciousness.

3 pounds assorted medium to large heirloom tomatoes
Kosher salt
6 ounces aged extra-sharp white cheddar cheese, shredded
½ cup mayonnaise
2 large shallots, chopped
3 cloves garlic, minced
1 large egg
¼ cup chopped fresh basil, plus more for garnish
¼ cup chopped fresh parsley
¼ cup thinly sliced green onion, green part only, plus more for garnish
1 tablespoon Dijon mustard
Salt and freshly ground black pepper
1 pre-baked 9-inch pie crust, store-bought or homemade

Preheat the oven to 400°F. Cut tomatoes into ½-inch slices. Salt 8 of the slices and allow them to drain on a paper-towel-lined plate. Meanwhile, place a wire rack over a cookie sheet. Arrange remaining tomato slices in one layer on the rack, and place in the oven to roast for 45 minutes. Cool completely.

Stir together cheese, mayonnaise, shallots, garlic, egg, basil, parsley, green onion, and Dijon mustard. Add salt and pepper to taste.

Spread ⅓ of the cheese mixture on the bottom of the pie crust. Layer on ½ of the roasted tomatoes. Make another layer of cheese mixture and arrange the remainder of the roasted tomatoes. Spread on one more layer of cheese and make the final top layer using the salt-dried tomatoes.

Bake pie until set, 40 to 45 minutes. Let cool 1 hour. Sprinkle with additional basil and green onion before serving.

WHITE BARBECUE SAUCE

BRENT ROSEN | MAKES ABOUT 1 CUP

White barbecue sauce uses mayonnaise as its base instead of the more traditional ketchup or mustard. Legendary Alabama pitmaster Big Bob Gibson introduced white sauce at his eponymous barbecue joint in Decatur in the early 1920s. Since then, barbecue lovers in north Alabama have been slathering their slow-smoked chicken in white sauce. In the early 2000s, white sauce escaped from north Alabama and into the wider southern consciousness, and it now appears alongside chicken wings, leg quarters, and sandwiches at barbecue joints around the Southeast.

This recipe uses Duke's Mayonnaise, the tangy, vinegary condiment created by South Carolina entrepreneur Eugenia Thomas Duke in the early 1900s. We also call for Tabasco's version of sriracha sauce for heat. Tabasco's original and internationally famous hot sauce was developed in Louisiana in 1868 by food lover Edmund McIlhenny on Avery Island, which is a three-mile salt dome surrounded by marsh.

1 cup mayonnaise (we prefer Duke's)
¼ cup apple cider vinegar
1 tablespoon Tabasco-brand sriracha sauce
1 teaspoon Worcestershire sauce
½ teaspoon celery seeds
¼ teaspoon crushed red pepper flakes
¼ teaspoon cayenne pepper
Kosher salt and freshly ground black pepper, to taste

Whisk all ingredients together; then season with salt and pepper. Cover and refrigerate up to 5 days.

KUMQUAT MARMALADE

ELIZABETH M. WILLIAMS | MAKES APPROXIMATELY 6 PINTS (BEGIN A DAY AHEAD)

7 cups water
3½ pound kumquats, washed and sliced (leave in the seeds)
1 cup lemon juice
8 cups granulated sugar

Thoroughly wash and rinse 6 pint jars and lids. Set them aside. Pour water into a large pot and add the prepared kumquats. Add the lemon juice. Bring the pot to a boil and stir well. Boil the kumquats 1 minute. Remove from the heat and stir in the sugar until it is dissolved. Cool thoroughly. Cover the pot and set aside overnight.

The next day, return the pot to the stove, and heat, uncovered, until the mixture simmers. Stir often to keep the fruit from sticking to the bottom. Cook over medium heat until a candy thermometer reaches 220°F. Do not allow it to reach a higher temperature. Another test for doneness is to place a teaspoon of the liquid on a plate and allow it to cool. It should be neither runny nor hard. If the liquid is too runny, cook 15 more minutes and try again. If it gets too hard, add a few tablespoons water and cook a few more minutes.

Remove the pot from the heat and ladle the marmalade into the clean jars. Cool to room temperature and store in the refrigerator.

SATSUMA-INFUSED WHITE NEGRONI

LAURA BELLUCCI | MAKES 1 COCKTAIL

Ice cubes
1¼ ounces gin
1 ounce white vermouth
¾ ounce Aveze Gentiane Liqueur
½ ounce satsuma juice
2 drops orange bitters
2 drops Angostura bitters
For serving: satsuma peel

To a large mixing glass filled with ice, add the gin, vermouth, Aveze, satsuma juice, and both bitters. Stir until well chilled. Strain into a rocks glass filled with large ice cubes. Garnish with a satsuma peel.

The Arkansas exhibit, highlighting a range of Arkansas food specialties.

ARKANSAS

EARLY NATIVES OF ARKANSAS were hunter-gatherers, eating game and foraging for edible plants. The beginnings of agriculture in what is now Arkansas centered on corn, squash, and beans; these foods formed the state's cultural food pattern. They were extremely important to Native American inhabitants, as reflected in their hierarchy, food rituals, and identifiable vessels, tools, and cooking methods. As European settlers arrived, they set up a European system of agriculture, raising their own traditional grains and developing trade up and down the Mississippi River. Yet the French and later the Spanish also ate the food of the Quapaw Native Americans—dining on smoked buffalo tongues, for example, washed down with French and Spanish wines. Despite the presence of French and Spanish Catholics, Arkansas became a predominantly Protestant area, and dinner was eaten cold on many Sundays, a day of rest.

The landscape was rocky, and the soil was poor, but eventually early pioneers from Kentucky, Illinois, and Tennessee, who were used to farming in difficult conditions, moved into Arkansas. They brought their own recipes for curing hams, roasting pork ribs over open fires, and baking soda biscuits and molasses cakes. By the mid-nineteenth century, cattle became a major industry, and the citizenry was eating beef; barbecue became a common cooking method. Enslaved Africans introduced okra and emphasized frying as a way to cook. In the 1840s, Arkansas farmers began experimenting with orchards. Apples and peaches became important fruit crops.

Food doesn't respect political borders, and the places where several states meet are always full of food that is lively and a little bit different. Arkansas cuisine, which borders the South, the Midwest, and the Southwest, has influences from the Mississippi Valley, Ozark hill cooking, and Texas/Oklahoma Mexican cuisine, making today's food in the state unique.

Traditional fare includes fried catfish along the Mississippi River, roast duck and candied yams in the southern bayou country, and Ozark hill country bread and apple jelly. Arkansans consume plenty of grits and rice, and everything is, as throughout the South, washed down with sweet tea.

A popular dessert is the Arkansas version of strawberry shortcake, which is a crisp buttery biscuit soaked in strawberry juice. Chocolate anything, including chocolate gravy, is a favorite. Who can look at a salad of pink tomatoes without thinking of Arkansas?

In the last fifty years Arkansas has become a major poultry state, with nationally known Tyson Foods operating in Springdale.

FRIED PICKLES

BRENT ROSEN | MAKES 12

Atkins, Arkansas, was home to the Atkins Pickle Plant for more than fifty years. In 1963, Bernell "Fatman" Austin, an Atkins restaurateur, decided to take advantage of the pickle plant across the street from his restaurant and introduced fried dill pickles to his menu. Although pickles had been fried before, it was Austin who dedicated the time, ingenuity, and effort to perfect the recipe. He chose to fry pickles sliced lengthwise, rather than the usual coins or wedges, to increase the batter-to-pickle ratio and make the pickles a better vehicle for sauces. The Atkins pickle factory closed in 2002, but the Austin family still comes together for two days each May for the Atkins Pickle Festival, where they fry the family's secret-recipe pickles. This recipe is inspired by Fatman Austin and his legendary Arkansas fried pickles.

Oil for deep frying
1 cup all-purpose flour
¼ teaspoon garlic powder
¼ teaspoon cayenne pepper
¼ teaspoon smoked paprika
1 teaspoon pepper
½ teaspoon salt
½ cup buttermilk
1 large egg
12 dill pickle slices, cut lengthwise from whole dill pickles (waffle-cut pickles hold the batter better)

In a large heavy pot or fryer, heat 2 inches oil to 375°F. In a medium bowl, mix together the flour, garlic powder, cayenne, paprika, pepper, and salt. In another bowl, whisk together the buttermilk and egg.

Pat pickles dry; dredge the slices first in the wet mix and then coat them in the dry mix. Drop a few slices at a time into the hot oil, and cook until golden brown, about 4 minutes. Flip once during cooking. Drain on paper towels and serve hot.

SMOKED TURKEY SALAD WITH BÉARNAISE DRESSING

ELIZABETH M. WILLIAMS | MAKES 6 SERVINGS

3 cups chopped smoked turkey
1 pint grapes, cut in half
1 cup chopped, toasted pecans or almonds
½ cup chopped celery
½ cup sliced scallions (white and green parts)
Béarnaise Dressing (recipe follows)
For serving: crackers, bread, or salad

Mix all salad ingredients together in a large bowl and toss thoroughly with the dressing. Serve with crackers or on bread or on a salad.

BÉARNAISE DRESSING

MAKES ABOUT 1 CUP

¾–1 cup mayonnaise
2 tablespoons chopped parsley
1 tablespoon chopped fresh tarragon
1–2 teaspoons Dijon mustard
1–2 teaspoons lemon juice
1–2 teaspoons honey
½ teaspoon salt
Freshly ground black pepper, to taste

Place all ingredients in a bowl and mix well. Add amounts of mayonnaise, mustard, lemon juice, and honey according to your taste preference.

JAMMY PINK TOMATO CHICKEN

MADDIE HAYES | MAKES 2 GENEROUS SERVINGS

The South Arkansas Vine Ripe Pink Tomato was once a major crop for Arkansas; the state produced more than 290,000 tons in 1959. Unfortunately, because of its delicate skin and short growing season, this tomato variety is not a good match for modern grocery stores. Locals, however, still enjoy the breed and celebrate the season with pink tomato festivals. They also buy these tomatoes at markets, and some grow their own.

2 bone-in, skin-on chicken breasts
2 bone-in, skin-on chicken legs
1 tablespoon kosher salt
1 teaspoon black pepper
4 tablespoons olive oil, divided
1 small to medium onion, diced
4 cloves garlic, minced
1 teaspoon red pepper flakes
½ cup red wine
2 tablespoons tomato paste
1 tablespoon fish sauce
4 pink tomatoes, chopped

Preheat the oven to 425°F. Season chicken all over with salt and pepper. Heat 2 tablespoons oil in a large Dutch oven over medium-high heat. Add chicken, skin side down, and cook, without moving, until the chicken is browned on the bottom, 5 to 8 minutes. Take the chicken out of the pan and let it rest on a plate.

Add onions to the same pot and cook over medium heat until translucent, 10 to 12 minutes. Add garlic and red pepper flakes and cook over medium-high heat until the mixture sizzles and is lightly caramelized, about 2 minutes. Deglaze with red wine, making sure to scrape up all the bits on the bottom of the pot. When the wine is almost evaporated, add tomato paste and cook until rust-colored, about 5 minutes. Stir in the fish sauce. Add the tomatoes and cook down until saucy, 20 to 30 minutes.

Nestle chicken back in the Dutch oven. Bake, covered, until chicken is almost cooked through, 20 to 25 minutes. Drizzle chicken with remaining 2 tablespoons oil. Return to the oven, and bake, uncovered, until tomatoes have become jammy, the chicken is golden brown, and a thermometer inserted into thickest portion of breast registers 160°F, 20 to 30 more minutes. Let the chicken rest in the pot for 10 minutes and serve.

If you cannot find pink tomatoes, this is still delicious with any fresh tomatoes.

DROP BISCUITS

ELIZABETH M. WILLIAMS | MAKES 12 LARGE BISCUITS

These biscuits are faster to make than rolled biscuits but are just as flaky.

2 cups all-purpose flour
1 tablespoon baking powder
1 teaspoon salt
1 teaspoon sugar (if you like your biscuits on the sweet side)
½ cup (1 stick) cold unsalted butter or cold lard, cut into small pieces, plus melted butter for the skillet and for finishing
¾–1 cup whole milk

Preheat the oven to 425°F. Butter a large cast-iron skillet and set aside. Place flour, baking powder, salt, and sugar into a bowl and whisk well to blend. Add the butter and use a pastry cutter or your fingers to blend the mixture until the texture feels like coarse sand. Add ¾ cup milk. Stir with a wooden spoon. The dough will be shaggy. If all the flour mixture will not incorporate, stir in the remaining ¼ cup of milk.

Drop the biscuits by the heaping tablespoonful into the prepared skillet. (If you want them beautifully uniform in size, drop from your preferred-size ice cream scoop.) For biscuits that are crispy on all sides, place them an inch apart. Or to keep the sides soft, make sure the biscuits touch each other when dropped.

Bake until brown, 15–20 minutes. Remove from the oven and brush with melted butter. Serve warm.

CHOCOLATE GRAVY

ELIZABETH M. WILLIAMS | MAKES 2 CUPS

Biscuits and chocolate gravy is a unique Arkansas breakfast. For this recipe, you can bake the biscuits fresh or use them from last night's dinner.

4 tablespoons cocoa powder
4 tablespoons sugar
4 tablespoons all-purpose flour
2 cups milk
For serving: Hot biscuits

In a medium bowl, whisk together the cocoa powder, sugar, and flour. Pour the milk into a saucepan, and slowly heat it until just below the boiling point. Keep a keen eye on the pot because the milk should not boil. Whisk in the cocoa mixture. Stir constantly until the gravy thickens, 2–3 minutes. Pour over hot biscuits.

FUDGY BROWNIES

STEPHANIE BOTTOM | MAKES 12–24, DEPENDING ON PAN SIZE

2 cups all-purpose flour
1½ teaspoons baking powder
½ teaspoon salt
1 cup (2 sticks) butter
12 ounces unsweetened chocolate, chopped
3 cups granulated sugar
6 large eggs
2 tablespoons vanilla extract
1 cup toffee pieces
1 cup white chocolate pieces
1 cup milk chocolate pieces

Preheat the oven to 350°F. Grease a 12×18-inch jellyroll pan for thin brownies or a 9×13-inch baking pan for thick brownies. Place the flour, baking powder, and salt in a large bowl and whisk together.

In a small saucepan over medium heat, thoroughly melt together the butter and the unsweetened chocolate, stirring occasionally. Cool 10 minutes.

In a large bowl, whisk together the sugar, eggs, and vanilla. Pour in the cooled chocolate mixture and whisk together. Pour the chocolate mixture into the dry ingredients and whisk together. Pour batter into the prepared pan. Sprinkle the top with the toffee, white chocolate, and milk chocolate pieces. Use a knife to shallowly drag through the top to partially combine the toppings into the batter.

Bake until a toothpick inserted in the middle comes out with moist crumbs, but is not wet with batter, about 25 minutes in the jellyroll pan or 55 minutes in the smaller baking pan. Cool fully before cutting into squares and removing from the pan.

MOUNTAIN VALLEY PUNCH

BRENT ROSEN | MAKES 36 CUPS

In 1871, the Mountain Valley Spring Water Company was formed near the town of Hot Springs to bottle and sell the mineral water from the area's natural springs. It is the oldest U.S. spring water company still in operation.

1 gallon chilled orange juice, no pulp
1 gallon chilled cranberry juice
4 cups chilled Mountain Valley Sparkling Water
20 leaves fresh basil, cut in chiffonade (leaves rolled together and finely sliced)
Ice cubes for serving

Mix all ingredients together in a punch bowl. Serve over ice, in Art Deco punch glasses if you have them.

PIMM'S CUP PUNCH

BRENT ROSEN | MAKES 96 (4-OUNCE) SERVINGS

This punch is not exactly a large-batch version of the classic cucumber-scented Pimm's Cup, but it's pretty close. It is a perfect pregame drink that will please almost anyone.

6 cups Pimm's #1
6 cups lemonade made with fresh lemons
3 cups sparkling water
3 cups Cucumber-Mint Simple Syrup (recipe follows)
1 unpeeled cucumber, sliced
Ice cubes
For serving: mint sprigs (optional)

In a large punch bowl, combine Pimm's, lemonade, sparkling water, and simple syrup. Float the cucumber slices on the top and add ice. Serve in punch cups with a sprig of mint.

CUCUMBER-MINT SIMPLE SYRUP

MAKES ABOUT 3 CUPS (BEGIN A DAY AHEAD)

3 cups granulated sugar
3 cups water
1 cup mint leaves
2 cucumbers, peeled and roughly chopped

Combine the sugar and water in a pot and simmer until the sugar has dissolved, 3–5 minutes. Cool to room temperature. Add the mint and press lightly with the back of a spoon to bruise the herb slightly. Add the cucumber. Refrigerate the mixture overnight. Strain out the solids and discard. Keep syrup in a tightly covered jar in the refrigerator.

The Congressional Club cookbook, bean pot, and menu from the House of Representatives Restaurant, on display in the Washington, DC, exhibit.

DISTRICT OF COLUMBIA

THE DISTRICT OF COLUMBIA, created to be the nation's capital, was carved from two southern states, Virginia and Maryland. Throughout the early history of the country, presidents, who almost all had substantial means, brought their family cooks with them to the White House. There was no presidential staff other than that privately maintained by each president.

George Washington, who was president before the White House was built, had a cook named Hercules, who was enslaved. Thomas Jefferson, whose culinary influence on America has been touted, also had an enslaved chef, James Hemings, who accompanied Jefferson to France. While there, Hemings trained to become a professional chef by apprenticing at fine restaurants. In large part, it was Hemings's talent and hard work that created Jefferson's reputation as a gourmet.

Early White House cooks were specialists in "hearth cooking," meaning they cooked over fires. To broil meats and bake vegetables properly, they therefore had to be knowledgeable about controlling embers and ashes in stoves and ovens. They were also skilled at picking various types of wood and fuel sources. Hardwoods such as oak, apple, and hickory burned evenly with a moderate heat and lasted a long time. Coal burned the hottest and lasted the longest.

Today the White House has three kitchens: the main kitchen, a pastry kitchen, and the Executive Residence family kitchen. These kitchens are used for daily meal preparation for presidential families and to create the cuisine for more formal entertaining, such as state dinners. The kitchens are service areas and not on view to the public. They are rarely photographed and are almost always busy.

Much is made in the press when modern administrations purchase presidential china. Although various presidents have ordered new china as earlier services became depleted, worn, or broken, the china used in today's White House belongs to the people. There is a China Room Collection of examples of dishes used in the White House over time. The first several presidents used their own dinnerware for public dinners. James Monroe ordered the first official White House china in 1817, which was the first china designed for the White House.

OYSTERS & MIGNONETTE SAUCE

BRENT ROSEN | MAKES ENOUGH SAUCE FOR 2 DOZEN OYSTERS

When it comes to dressing oysters, mignonette is cocktail sauce's urbane cousin. A classic mignonette of vinegar and shallots provides a delicate, bright, and sophisticated accompaniment to oysters without overwhelming their natural essence. Mignonette is particularly delicious with farm-raised oysters, which often have more delicate, herbaceous, and vegetal qualities than the typical robust-flavored, bottom-raised Gulf oyster. When you are serving delicately flavored oysters, don't cover up the taste with ketchup and horseradish; enhance it with mignonette.

½ cup chopped shallots (3 or 4 large shallots)
¼ cup red wine vinegar
¼ cup champagne vinegar
⅛ teaspoon sugar
⅛ teaspoon kosher salt
1¼ teaspoons finely crushed white or pink peppercorns (do not use powdered; crush your own)
2 dozen freshly shucked oysters

Finely mince the chopped shallots in a food processor. Put the minced shallots in a medium bowl. Make sure to scrape in all the shallot juice, which adds flavor to the final sauce.

To the bowl, stir in the vinegars, sugar, and kosher salt. Use a fork to stir in the crushed peppercorns. Cover the sauce and chill at least 4 hours and up to 1 month. (The longer it sits, the better it tastes.) When serving your raw oysters, serve the mignonette in a metal ramekin with a demitasse spoon.

HALF-SMOKE SAUSAGE WITH CHILI CHEESE

ELIZABETH M. WILLIAMS | MAKES 8 SANDWICHES

Ben and Virginia Ali opened Ben's Chili Bowl, an important landmark of the DC culinary scene, in 1958. The restaurant is known for its chili dogs, milkshakes, and half-smokes, which are larger and spicier versions of hot dogs. In its early days, many famous jazz artists went to Ben's Chili Bowl when they performed at the nearby U Street clubs. The restaurant was also popular among both police and protestors during the 1968 riots that followed the assassination of Martin Luther King Jr.

From the 1970s until the 1990s, economic activity stagnated in the neighborhood, but Ben's Chili Bowl persevered. Today, Ben's Chili Bowl is still run by the Ali family and continues to play a significant role in DC dining establishments. Barack Obama ate there ten days before his presidential inauguration in 2009.

Though Washington, DC, is often considered a city without a unique food culture, ask anyone in the District and they'll cite half-smokes—spicy, chili-topped sausages—as the signature street food of our nation's capital. You can buy versions of it from the food trucks along the National Mall and in restaurants all over town. The etymology of the name is unclear, but many claim that it comes from the mixture of meats inside—half pork, half beef—and was a way to make sure that the sausage's origins weren't suspect. Half-smokes first appeared in the 1930s but didn't really take hold until the 1950s, when fast food gained traction.

CHILI SAUCE

3 tablespoons vegetable oil
¼ cup tomato paste
10 ounces twice-ground beef
1 onion, finely chopped
1 tablespoon, plus 2 teaspoons prepared chili powder
1 teaspoon cumin
1 teaspoon prepared yellow mustard
¼ teaspoon cayenne
1 clove garlic, minced
1 bay leaf
2 tablespoons flour
2 cups beef stock
2 tablespoons apple cider vinegar

Place the oil in a large saucepan over medium heat. Add the tomato paste and cook until it begins to caramelize, about 5 minutes. Add the ground beef and use a wooden spoon to stir it well and keep it from clumping. Cook 10 minutes.

Add the onion and cook 10 more minutes, stirring occasionally. Add the chili powder, cumin, mustard, cayenne, garlic, and bay leaf. Cook 3 more minutes. Sprinkle the flour into the pan and stir 2 minutes. Add the stock and vinegar. Stir until the sauce begins to thicken, about 10 more minutes. Reduce heat to keep the sauce warm. If it becomes too thick, dilute with additional chicken stock.

Assembly

8 half-smoke sausages*
8 hot dog buns, preferably a good potato roll
Yellow mustard
For serving: chopped raw onions

Grill the sausages. Spread the buns with yellow mustard. Add one half-smoke to each bun. Top with the chili sauce and garnish with raw onions.

*Half-smoke sausages are unique to the greater Washington, DC, area. You can buy them on the internet or just substitute regular hot dogs, which lack that smoky flavor but will still be tasty.

SENATE BEAN SOUP

SENATE KITCHEN | MAKES 8 SERVINGS

This dish is available in the U.S. Senate dining room every day. Although there are many apocryphal but uncorroborated stories that explain this tradition, the reason for the regularity of the dish's offering remains a mystery. On September 14, 1943, war rationing and a lack of beans made it impossible to prepare the soup. The next day, somehow enough beans were found to make the dish. Every day since then it has been on the menu, without interruption.

2 pounds dried navy beans
4 quarts hot water
1½ pounds smoked ham hocks
1 large onion, chopped
2 tablespoons butter
Salt and pepper to taste

Put the beans in a colander and run hot water through them until they turn slightly white. Place beans into a large pot with the hot water. Add ham hocks and simmer, covered, until tender, about 3 hours. Stir occasionally.

Remove ham hocks and set aside to cool. Dice the meat and return to the soup. Lightly brown the onion in the butter. Add to the soup. Before serving, bring the soup to a boil and season with salt and pepper.

GEORGETOWN-INSPIRED CHOCOLATE CUPCAKES

JENNIE MERRILL BOUDREAUX | MAKES 12

1 cup all-purpose flour
½ cup granulated sugar
½ cup light brown sugar, packed
6 tablespoons unsweetened cocoa powder
2 teaspoons baking powder
½ teaspoon salt
½ cup buttermilk
⅓ cup neutral vegetable oil, like canola or peanut oil
1 teaspoon vanilla extract or vanilla paste
2 large eggs
½ cup hot water
Chocolate Buttercream Frosting (recipe follows)

Preheat the oven to 350°F. Place muffin cup liners into a 12-cup muffin tin. In a large bowl, mix together the flour, sugars, cocoa powder, baking powder, and salt. Stir in buttermilk, oil, and vanilla. Add eggs, one at a time, stirring after each addition.

Add hot water and stir until combined. The batter should be thin. Fill muffin cup liners just over ⅔ of the way full. Bake until centers spring back when lightly touched, 18 to 22 minutes. Cool completely and then spread on chocolate buttercream frosting.

CHOCOLATE BUTTERCREAM FROSTING

MAKES ABOUT 2 CUPS

½ cup (1 stick) salted butter, at room temperature
2 cups powdered sugar
¼ cup cocoa powder
½ teaspoon vanilla extract
1 to 4 tablespoons milk

With a handheld mixer or a stand mixer fitted with a whisk attachment, beat the butter on medium-high speed until light colored, about 3 minutes. Using a low mixer speed, add the powdered sugar one cup at a time, and mix until completely combined.

Stir in the cocoa powder and then the vanilla extract. Add milk one tablespoon at a time and stir until frosting reaches spreading consistency.

JAMES HEMINGS'S FRENCH VANILLA ICE CREAM

ASHBELL MCELVEEN | MAKES 8–10 SERVINGS

Chef James Hemings, a slave of Thomas Jefferson, trained at the Chateau Chantilly and with master pastry chefs in Paris. Chateau Chantilly was considered the best table in prerevolutionary France, with food that was widely considered better than the food at Versailles.

On June 20, 1790, Chef Hemings cooked the most famous dinner in colonial America, the Assumption Dinner, which reconciled bitter enemies Alexander Hamilton and Thomas Jefferson. Jefferson used Hemings's skill as a master chef as a political weapon, and it worked. After the dinner Hamilton and Jefferson agreed that Washington would be the nation's capital and that states would assume the federal debt from the Revolutionary War.

Chef Hemings concluded the dinner with a stunning dessert: warm pastry stuffed with French-style vanilla ice cream. At the time, ice cream was being made in colonial America, but its consistency was that of a thick milkshake. French vanilla ice cream contains egg yolks, which give a smooth finish and allow for more consistent freezing. James Hemings was the first chef to introduce firm ice cream to America. Despite his culinary accomplishments, his legacy remains a ghost in America's kitchens.

6 large egg yolks, preferably organic
½ pound refined raw sugar
2 quarts heavy cream, preferably organic
1 whole vanilla bean
½ teaspoon salt

In a large bowl, whisk together the egg yolks and sugar until smooth, and set aside. In a large saucepan set over medium heat, add the cream and vanilla bean, and bring to near boiling. (Do not let it come to a boil.)

Remove the pot from the heat. Remove the vanilla bean and use a small sharp knife to split it down the length of the bean. Scrape seeds from the pod with the back of a knife and add the seeds back into the hot cream mixture.

In a slow, thin stream, add the hot cream mixture to the egg and sugar mixture, stirring constantly with a wooden spoon. Transfer the mixture to a double boiler and heat gently, stirring continually with a wooden spoon until the mixture thickens enough to coat the spoon. Transfer the custard to a bowl and cool completely at room temperature. Chill thoroughly in the refrigerator.

Freeze the chilled custard using your desired method: traditional churn, electric ice cream machine, or freezer trays. (Always make ice cream in small batches to assure quality.)

PRESIDENTIAL BARBECUE SAUCE

PRESIDENT DWIGHT D. EISENHOWER | MAKES 2 CUPS

The Eisenhower Center in Abilene, Kansas, which houses the presidential library of Dwight D. Eisenhower, offers this recipe from the thirty-fourth president's personal collection. He was born in Texas, and this recipe reflects the Texas barbecue tradition.

20 ounces canned tomatoes, drained and sieved (should have 2 cups)
4 tablespoons (½ stick) butter
1 small yellow onion, finely chopped
¼ cup vinegar
1 tablespoon sugar
1 tablespoon paprika
2 teaspoons salt
2 teaspoons chili powder
1½ teaspoons Worcestershire sauce
1 teaspoon ground black pepper
¼ teaspoon Tabasco sauce or more, to taste

Combine all the ingredients in a medium saucepan. Bring to a simmer over medium heat and cook, stirring occasionally, for 15 minutes. Use for basting up to 5 pounds of meat or chicken. Can also be served as a table sauce.

Photo courtesy of Buffalo & Bergen.

LOX'D & LOADED (BLOODY MARY INCLUDED)

GINA CHERSEVANI | MAKES 1 SERVING

Washington, DC, barkeep Gina Chersevani invented this cocktail and bagel sandwich/garnish combo, which some declare is the perfect hangover cure.

LOADED BLOODY MARY

2 ounces vodka or gin
4 ounces Bloody Mary Mix (recipe follows)
4 ounces freshly squeezed lemon juice
Ice cubes

Place all ingredients into a shaker filled with ice. Shake well and transfer with ice to a tall glass.

BLOODY MARY MIX

MAKES A PITCHER (ABOUT 6 TO 8 DRINKS)

4 cups tomato juice (recipe follows)
2 tablespoons ground black pepper, plus more if needed
1 ounce freshly grated horseradish
4 ounces Tabasco sauce
2 ounces sriracha sauce
2 ounces freshly squeezed lemon juice
2 ounces Worcestershire sauce
2 tablespoons whole celery seed
Salt, to taste

Place all ingredients in a tall pitcher and stir well. Adjust for salt and pepper.

TOMATO JUICE

MAKES 4 CUPS

3 pounds ripe, juicy tomatoes
1 onion, roughly chopped
2 tablespoons salt

Place all ingredients in a stainless-steel pot and simmer 30 minutes. The tomatoes should be broken down and the onion soft. Remove from heat and allow the mixture to cool until almost room temperature. In a food processor, process in batches until completely smooth. Mixture will be thick. Strain through a fine strainer or the fine disk of a food mill. Reserve solids for another use.

LOX'D BAGEL

1 bagel, sliced
Cream cheese, to taste
3 ounces lox
Capers, to taste
Red onion slices, to taste
1 lettuce leaf
1 lemon slice
1 pitted green olive
1 long toothpick

Generously spread the two cut sides of the bagel with cream cheese. Divide the lox between the two bagel halves. Sprinkle with capers and onion slices. Press the two halves of the bagel together to form a sandwich. To serve with panache, place the lettuce leaf on top of the glass of the Lox'd and Loaded cocktail. Place the bagel on the lettuce leaf. Garnish with the lemon slice and the olive, secured on a toothpick.

CLASSIC GIN MARTINI

THE MUSEUM OF THE AMERICAN COCKTAIL

MAKES 1 COCKTAIL

The martini is the quintessential cocktail; however, its recipe has fluctuated wildly over the years. We feel that this version represents a return to its roots as a well-balanced drink. Although you may adjust the ratio of gin to vermouth to suit your tastes, we recommend that you try it this way at least once to see how you like it.

The origin of the martini is unclear. The earliest known martini recipe appears in Harry Johnson's 1888 book, *New and Improved Bartenders' Manual.* The drink itself appeared in newspapers as early as 1883, where its precise composition was already being debated.

1½ ounces gin
½ ounce dry vermouth
1 dash orange bitters
Ice cubes
For serving: lemon twist or green olive

Stir the drink ingredients together in a large glass filled with ice. Strain into a chilled cocktail glass. Garnish with a lemon twist or green olive.

A Cuban coffee stand in the Florida exhibit.

FLORIDA

FLORIDA, THE LARGE, SUNNY, SUBTROPICAL peninsula poised at the southeasternmost corner of the United States, has the distinction of being bordered by both the Gulf of Mexico and the Atlantic Ocean. Florida's environment provides the perfect ecology for native seafoods, such as conch, oysters, shrimp, crabs, clams, and many varieties of fin fish. The islands at the southern tip of the peninsula, the Keys, are an important connection to the Caribbean, with its distinctive food and culture that have spread throughout the state.

Tropical fruits such as coconut, mangos, bananas, and plantains can be found in dishes like mofongo and mango salad. Sugar production is a major industry, with sugarcane fields extending for thousands of acres around South Beach County. Florida is a major supplier of agricultural products to the country, and its legendary citrus production has transformed the breakfast tables of America.

Various waves of immigration have influenced Florida's food. Traditional Jewish cuisine, midwestern foods such as casseroles, and corporate fast foods are all part of its food scene. Cuban coffee, rum, fruit drinks, and key lime pie are easily recognizable as part of Florida's table. Tupperware, a transformative industrial product for American women, has long called Florida home.

CEVICHE

BRENT ROSEN | MAKES 8 APPETIZER SERVINGS

Ceviche is raw fish cured in citrus juice to create a light, bright appetizer or snack. Restaurants throughout coastal Florida specialize in ceviche, using the excellent fish that swim off its coasts. You can use any firm white fish, such as snapper, sea bass, grouper, or, as we suggest, mahi-mahi. Our recipe includes jalapeños, tomatoes, and avocados, so the ceviche has plenty of sweet, spicy, and creamy flavors to go along with the cured fish.

2 pounds firm white fish, such as mahi-mahi, cut into ½-inch chunks
½ cup freshly squeezed lime juice
½ cup freshly squeezed lemon juice
½ red onion, diced
1 cup tomatoes, chopped
1 large avocado, small diced
1 fresh jalapeño pepper, chopped
2 teaspoons salt
Dash each dried oregano and cayenne pepper
Dash of Tabasco Original Hot Sauce (red)
For serving: soda crackers, tortilla chips, or toast points

In a glass or stainless-steel bowl, gently mix together fish, lime juice, and lemon juice. Cover and refrigerate at least 4 hours and as long as overnight.

When ready to serve, add remaining ingredients and toss to combine. Serve with soda crackers, tortilla chips, or toast points.

CUBAN SANDWICH

BRENT ROSEN MAKES 4 SANDWICHES

The debate over the origins of the Cuban sandwich is as hot as the fresh-from-the-press "Cubano" itself. Cubans in Tampa say the popular sandwich is their contribution to culinary culture and that it was invented by their original ethnic community working in Florida's cigar factories. Cubans in Miami would beg to differ, arguing that south Florida is the capital of Cuban culture in America and that the sandwich was first served in south, not west, Florida. Regardless of which claim you believe, there is no denying that the addition of roasted pork, pickles, and mustard makes this gussied-up ham-and-cheese one of the South's most delicious sandwiches.

PORK FILLING

1 pound pork tenderloin, trimmed of extra fat and silverskin
½ cup freshly squeezed orange juice
½ cup freshly squeezed lime juice
¼ cup chopped cilantro
2 cloves garlic, finely chopped
1 tablespoon light brown sugar
2 teaspoons salt
1 teaspoon cumin
1 teaspoon freshly ground black pepper
1 teaspoon smoked paprika
1 teaspoon dried oregano

Place pork in a nonreactive dish. Combine remaining ingredients and pour over the pork. Marinate it in the refrigerator for at least 4 hours and up to overnight.

When ready to bake, preheat the oven to 450°F. Remove the pork from the marinade and pat dry. Roast the pork, uncovered, in the oven until an instant-read thermometer reaches 140°F, about 20–25 minutes. Remove from oven and let the pork rest at least 5 minutes before slicing.

Sandwich Assembly

4 Cuban sandwich loaves or pistolettes, cut in half lengthwise
½ cup (1 stick) unsalted butter, softened
4 large dill pickles, thinly sliced
1 cup yellow mustard
1 pound thick-sliced honey ham
Roast pork (recipe above)
16 slices Swiss cheese

To make sandwiches, rub the outside of the bread with butter, and place on a cutting board, buttered side down. On the bottom half of each bread roll, layer the pickles, mustard, ham, roast pork, and Swiss cheese. Place tops on sandwiches, buttered side out.

Heat a panini maker or sandwich press until warm.* Press sandwiches in batches until they are hot and the cheese is melted, about 5 minutes. Cut sandwiches diagonally and serve.

*If you do not have a panini press, try using a waffle iron, which makes interesting impressions on the surface of the bread. Wrap the entire sandwich in aluminum foil and press in the waffle iron. You can also lay the sandwich in a hot, heavy cast-iron or aluminum skillet and press down on it with a smaller hot skillet.

CONCH FRITTERS & AIOLI

BYRON BRADLEY | MAKES 4 SERVINGS

Conch, a marine mollusk, is a staple of southern Florida cuisine. This sea snail is such a pervasive icon in culinary and local culture that Key West natives have nicknamed themselves "conchs." Conch is usually served fried in a fritter or raw in a salad. Fresh or frozen conch can be found in many coastal grocery stores. It can also be bought frozen on the internet.

1 pound fresh conch
½ Scotch bonnet pepper, habanero, or jalapeño, chopped fine
½ cup minced onion
1 stalk celery, minced
½ green bell pepper, minced
½ red bell pepper, minced
2 large eggs
1 teaspoon fresh thyme
1½ cups all-purpose flour
¾ teaspoon baking powder
¾ teaspoon curry powder
¾ teaspoon salt
¼ teaspoon freshly cracked black pepper
½ cup club soda
½ cup beer
6 cups peanut oil for frying
For serving: Aioli (recipe follows)

Place the conch on a cutting board or other tough work surface. Use the rough side of a meat mallet to pound the conch to about ¼ inch thick. Use a very sharp knife to mince the conch into a ¼-inch dice. Transfer to the bowl of a food processor and pulse 10 to 15 times. Transfer the minced conch to a large mixing bowl, and add the hot pepper, onion, celery, bell pepper, eggs, and thyme. Stir to combine. Set aside.

In another bowl, whisk together the flour, baking powder, curry powder, salt, and pepper. Add the flour mixture to the conch and stir until well combined. Add the club soda and beer; stir until combined. The mixture should be thick.

Heat the peanut oil in an electric deep fryer to 350°F. From just above the oil's surface, use a ⅛-cup scoop to gently drop in the batter, being careful not to spatter the oil. Don't crowd the fryer. The fritters will sink to the bottom and then float to the top. Cook, turning occasionally, until golden brown, 4–5 minutes. Use a slotted spoon or spider to transfer the fritters to a paper-lined baking sheet. Work in batches until all the fritter batter is fried. Serve immediately with the aioli.

AIOLI

MAKES 1 CUP

1 cup mayonnaise
2 tablespoons freshly squeezed key lime or Persian lime juice
1–2 teaspoons of your favorite hot sauce
½ teaspoon lime zest
½ teaspoon salt

Combine all the ingredients in a small bowl. Whisk to combine and refrigerate.

SAUTÉED TUNA WITH AVOCADO & MANGO SALAD

JULIA JOHNSTON | MAKES 2 SERVINGS

To keep things as fresh as possible, make the avocado and mango salad and the vinaigrette just before searing the tuna.

TUNA

3 tablespoons canola oil or other neutral oil
1 teaspoon sesame oil
¾ pound yellowfin tuna steaks
Salt and pepper
½ cup sesame seeds
Avocado & Mango Salad (recipe follows)
Vinaigrette (recipe follows)
For serving: macadamia nuts and plantain chips

Stir together canola and sesame oils. Brush the tuna with the oil mixture. Sprinkle with salt and pepper, and press sesame seeds onto all sides. Heat a nonstick or cast-iron skillet over high heat until very hot. Sear the tuna so that it is crusted on the outside but raw to warm on the inside, 30–45 second on each side.

To serve, plate the Avocado & Mango Salad. Place the tuna on the plate with the salad. Sprinkle the plate with macadamia nuts and top with the vinaigrette. Serve with plantain chips.

AVOCADO & MANGO SALAD

1 mango, peeled and chopped
1 avocado, peeled and chopped
1 tablespoon freshly squeezed lime juice
10 macadamia nuts, chopped
1 jalapeño, diced (optional)

Sprinkle the mango and avocado with lime juice. Stir in the chopped nuts and jalapeño.

VINAIGRETTE

2 tablespoons sugar
¼ cup water
2½ tablespoons white vinegar
¼ teaspoon salt
¼ teaspoon red pepper flakes

In a small saucepan set over low heat, dissolve the sugar in the water. Remove from heat, place the liquid in a small bowl or jar, and stir in vinegar, salt, and pepper flakes. Cool to room temperature.

TENNESSEE WILLIAMS'S KEY LIME PIE

BRINLEY RHYS & HIS GRANDMOTHER MAMA LEA

MAKES AN 8-INCH PIE

Mama Lea claimed that this recipe was a favorite of Tennessee Williams. She says she received it from a friend of the famous playwright. If that isn't the truth, it certainly is a treasured part of family lore.

1 cup granulated sugar
¾ cup lime zest
½ cup, plus 1 tablespoon key lime juice
½ cup (1 stick) butter
4 large eggs, beaten
1 (8-inch) baked graham cracker pie crust, homemade or purchased
For serving: whipped cream

Prepare a double boiler over a medium-low flame. Put the sugar, lime zest, lime juice, and butter into the top of the boiler, and cook until the butter has melted, stirring often. Gradually add the beaten eggs, straining them into the mixture to avoid them scrambling. (You can blend the eggs and the lime juice in a blender and then combine the mixture with the rest of the filling ingredients. This method tends to be easier than straining.)

Bring to a boil and cook until thick, stirring constantly, about 10 minutes. Cool to room temperature, then pour into the pie shell. Chill at least 6 hours. Cover with whipped cream just before serving.

WATERMELON RIND PICKLES

ELIZABETH M. WILLIAMS | MAKES ABOUT 2 QUARTS

1 cup apple cider vinegar
1 cup water
¾ cup granulated sugar
½ cup sliced ginger
10 whole black peppercorns
10 allspice berries
5 cardamom pods
2 pounds clean watermelon rind, cut into 1-inch cubes

Place the vinegar, water, and sugar in a large pot. Stir to make sure the sugar dissolves, and heat until the mixture begins to boil. Add the ginger and spices. Bring to a boil and cook 2 minutes; then carefully add the watermelon rind. Bring to a boil and cook 1 minute. Remove from heat and cool 5 minutes.

Pack the watermelon rind into a clean 2-quart jar. Using a funnel, ladle the liquid and spices into the jar. (Use a second jar if necessary.) Refrigerate the filled jar for 3 days. The pickles must be consumed within 30 days and must be kept refrigerated.

MOJITO

THE MUSEUM OF THE AMERICAN COCKTAIL

MAKES 1 COCKTAIL

This drink owes its fame to the bar La Bodeguita del Medio in Havana. Its claim that Ernest Hemingway was a regular patron and a fan of its mojitos has been dismissed as a marketing ploy by many, including Hemingway cocktail expert Philip Greene. Although Hemingway tended to write about drinks and bars he favored, he never mentioned the mojito or La Bodeguita in any of his letters or works.

2 teaspoons bar sugar (or 1 ounce simple syrup), plus additional for serving
8–12 mint leaves
2 ounces soda water, divided
Ice cubes
1½ ounces light rum
¾ ounce fresh lime juice
2 quarters of a whole lime peel (saved from squeezing the lime juice)
For serving: a fresh mint sprig

Place sugar, mint, and a splash of soda in a pint glass. Muddle together the sugar and the mint. Add ice to the glass; then add rum, lime juice, and the two lime peel quarters. Shake well and then strain into an ice-filled glass. Top with remaining soda. Garnish with a mint sprig and sprinkle with sugar.

HEMINGWAY DAIQUIRI

THE MUSEUM OF THE AMERICAN COCKTAIL

MAKES 1 COCKTAIL

Museum of the American Cocktail cofounder Philip Greene, author of *To Have and Have Another: A Hemingway Cocktail Companion,* says that this drink first appeared on the 1937 menu of the Bar Florida (aka the Floridita) in Havana, going by the (misspelled) name "E. Henmiway Special." By the mid-1940s, Florida resident Hemingway preferred a double-sized version, which became known as the "Papa Doble." Hemingway disdained sugar, so if you find this version a bit tart, add a little simple syrup.

1½ cups crushed ice
2 ounces white rum
½ ounce lime juice
1 teaspoon grapefruit juice
1 teaspoon maraschino liqueur

Frappe (finely crush) the ice in a blender. Pour remaining ingredients into the blender, and blend until smooth, about 15 seconds. Pour into a coupe glass. (If you don't have a blender, crush ice extremely fine and shake everything vigorously in a shaker.)

Coca-Cola, the Varsity, Big Green Egg, and peaches from the Georgia exhibit.

GEORGIA

KNOWN AS THE PEACH STATE, Georgia produces more than forty types of the fruit, which benefit from the state's long growing season.

Black-eyed peas, cream peas, crowder peas, okra, and greens reflect the state's African American heritage. Squash, beans, and corn reflect its Native American influence. As in most of the South, different regions of the state are known for different specialties. Those along the Atlantic coast, for example, feast on oysters, shrimp, fish, and crabs. Low-country Georgia gives us its version of Frogmore stew, made with shrimp, sausage, potatoes, and corn.

Before the arrival of Europeans, Cherokees and Creeks living in what is now Georgia cultivated corn. Many corn dishes are still popular: grits, hushpuppies, corndodgers, cornbread, and corn pudding. Corn flour flavors and crisps fried foods, especially fish. Tomato-based Brunswick stew is popular in Georgia and is typically served with a side of cornbread.

Georgia has a large peanut industry. A few popular local dishes include boiled peanuts, peanut brittle, peanut cake, peanut pie, and peanut butter. Pecans, the native tree nut, are spiced, candied, and baked into pies. Scuppernongs, a grape variety called Sculpins, and Muscadine grapes find their way into juice, jams, and jellies. Sweet potatoes, blueberries, fried green tomatoes, biscuits, red-eye gravy, sweet tea, and buttermilk all grace many a Georgia table.

Georgia is the home of Coca-Cola, the soft drink that has come to represent the United States in many places overseas. Today the company includes many other soda brands, as well as bottled water and juices. Flowers, another company headquartered in Georgia, is one of the country's largest bakeries, with locations across the United States.

BOILED PEANUTS

SERIGNE MBAYE | MAKES 10 SERVINGS (BEGIN A DAY AHEAD)

Georgia is the largest grower of peanuts in the United States, producing almost half of the nation's harvest annually, and has named the humble peanut as its official state crop. Although other states boast of peanut pioneers such as George Washington Carver and the creation of foods such as peanut butter and boiled peanuts, Georgia is best known for the legume. The state hosts its annual Peanut Festival every October in Sylvester.

4 cups raw "green" peanuts
Water for soaking, plus 3 cups
½ cup white wine vinegar
½ cup brown sugar
3 tablespoons kosher salt
½ teaspoon crushed red pepper
4 cloves garlic
1 habanero pepper (optional)

In a large bowl, cover the raw, unshelled peanuts with water and let them soak overnight.

Thoroughly rinse peanuts and add them and the remaining ingredients to a large pot. Make sure peanuts are completely submerged. Bring to a boil, cover the pot, and reduce the heat to a low boil. Cook until peanuts are soft, about 2–3 hours, adding water as needed to keep peanuts covered. Drain and serve hot.

VIDALIA ONION DIP

MADDIE HAYES | MAKES 3 CUPS

Vidalia onions are sweet, relatively flat-shaped yellow onions that have been growing in a legally designated production area of twenty South Georgia counties since 1986. These onions owe their sweetness to the region's special soil, which is low in sulfur.

In the 1930s, farmers in the Vidalia, Georgia, area decided to grow onions as a cash crop. They were quickly disappointed when they discovered their onions were not pungent but instead were high in sugar content. Success came later through the creation of a farmer's market located between Macon, Augusta, and Savannah, which helped spread these atypical onions throughout the state. Vidalia onions also increased in circulation when a Piggly Wiggly grocery store opened in Vidalia and began selling them. Festivals in Glennville and Vidalia, as well as a Vidalia Onion Museum, were created to promote Vidalia onions. In 1990, the Vidalia onion became Georgia's official state vegetable.

2 tablespoons olive oil
2 large Vidalia onions, sliced ⅛ inch thick
2–4 garlic cloves, minced
½–1 teaspoon chopped fresh thyme
Salt and pepper, to taste
16 ounces sour cream
1 tablespoon lemon juice
For serving: chopped chives and rippled or kettle-cooked potato chips

Heat oil in a skillet over medium heat. Cook the onion until just translucent, stirring occasionally, about three minutes. Add garlic, thyme, salt, and pepper. Cook, stirring occasionally, until the onion is caramelized and very soft, 35–40 minutes. Remove from heat, put in a large bowl, and let cool.

Mix the sour cream and lemon juice in the bowl of onions. Check for seasoning. Refrigerate at least 30 minutes to allow the flavors to come together. When ready to serve, garnish with chives and serve with potato chips. Can be made a day ahead and kept covered in the refrigerator.

BRUNSWICK STEW

MIKIE HAYES | MAKES 10 SERVINGS

Brunswick stew is usually tomato based, with meat and other vegetables. As with most traditional dishes, there is no one exact recipe. Brunswick County, Virginia, and the town of Brunswick, Georgia, both claim to have invented the dish, though there are a few differences between the two versions. The Georgia version was reportedly invented in 1898 on St. Simons Island. Georgia Brunswick stew tends to contain beef and pork, rather than the chicken and rabbit typically found in the Virginia version. Brunswick stew is associated with barbecues and fundraisers and is a mainstay of family reunions.

This recipe includes instructions for making shredded pork. If you want to save time, you can use prepared pulled pork or pork barbecue. A good substitute is shredded beef brisket.

6 tablespoons butter
1½ cups chopped sweet onion
1 tablespoon chopped fresh garlic
3 cups chicken stock
3 cups diced potatoes (round red or white are best)
2 cups corn kernels
1 (14½-ounce) can petite-cut diced tomatoes
1½ cups frozen baby lima beans
2 cups Shredded Pork (recipe follows)
2 cups Shredded Chicken (recipe follows)
1½ cups of your favorite prepared tomato-based barbecue sauce
3 tablespoons brown sugar, packed
1 tablespoon white vinegar
1 teaspoon salt
½ teaspoon ground black pepper
½ teaspoon ground cayenne pepper
For serving: plain, sweet, or jalapeño cornbread or buttermilk biscuits

Melt the butter in a large Dutch oven over medium heat. Add the onion and sauté, stirring frequently, until the onion is translucent but not caramelized, about 8 minutes. Add the garlic and sauté 2 minutes. Add the chicken stock, potatoes, corn, tomatoes, and lima beans. Bring to a boil; then cover, reduce heat, and simmer until potatoes are tender, about 30 minutes.

Add the shredded pork, shredded chicken, barbecue sauce, brown sugar, vinegar, salt, black pepper, and cayenne pepper. Combine well and simmer, uncovered, until heated through, 15 minutes. Serve hot in bowls with a side of cornbread or biscuits.

SHREDDED PORK

MAKES ABOUT 2 CUPS (BEGIN A DAY AHEAD)

A 2½- to 3-pound pork shoulder, at room temperature
Salt and pepper
2 medium sweet onions like a Vidalia, quartered
4 carrots, quartered
1½ cups beef broth, water, unsweetened apple juice, or beer (or enough to cover roast)
2 tablespoons Worcestershire sauce
1 tablespoon hot sauce
1 tablespoon onion powder
1 tablespoon garlic powder
½ tablespoon ground cumin

The night before you make the stew, cook the pork in a crockpot. Season the room-temperature pork generously with salt and pepper, and place it, fat side up, in the crockpot. Arrange the onions and carrots around the bottom of the roast. Whisk together the broth, Worcestershire sauce, hot sauce, onion powder, garlic powder, and cumin. Pour the mixture over the roast. Cover the pot and cook on low until the center of the pork registers 165°F on a digital thermometer, about 8–10 hours. Check periodically to make sure the broth hasn't evaporated. Cool the pork and shred.

SHREDDED CHICKEN

MAKES ABOUT 2 CUPS (CAN BE MADE A DAY AHEAD)

1 tablespoon olive oil
4 boneless, skinless chicken breasts, or 6 boneless, skinless thighs
Salt and pepper, to taste
¾ cup chicken broth

Drizzle the olive oil into a large sauté pan set over medium heat. Add the chicken and generously sprinkle it with salt and pepper. Cook until slightly golden on one side, about 5 minutes. With tongs, flip chicken. Add the broth to the pan and cover with a lid. Cook until a digital meat thermometer inserted into the center of the meat reads 165°F, about 10 minutes. Cool the chicken and shred it.

VARSITY-STYLE SMASH BURGER

BRENT ROSEN   MAKES 4 BURGERS

Found mostly in diners and fast-food restaurants, smash burger meat is mashed against a griddle so that the fat renders and crisps the outside. The Varsity Restaurant in Atlanta inspired this version of the burger. If you want to make yours taste more like the Varsity's, top your cooked burger with bean-free chili.

1 pound ground beef (80% lean, 20% fat)
American cheese
4 hamburger buns
Toppings of your choice

Heat a cast-iron skillet or griddle on high heat for at least 5 minutes. Divide the beef into 4 equal-sized balls. Do not over-handle the meat, or the burger will be tough. Place 2 balls of meat in the hot skillet, and mash them down with another skillet until the balls are flat and about the same diameter as your bun. Season generously with salt and pepper. Cook 1 minute.

Use a heavy spatula to carefully scrape the burgers from the skillet, making sure to get up all the browned bits. Flip the burgers and immediately place cheese on the tops. Cook another minute; then remove from the skillet. Repeat with the other two burgers. Place patties on buns and top with your favorite toppings.

SOUTHERN BISCUITS

BRENT ROSEN | MAKES 12 BISCUITS

The best mornings start with a pile of flaky, layered, golden-brown biscuits. Biscuits are one of the foods that inspire vehement debate among southerners, with partisans arguing over which state has the best ones. The Carolinas, Tennessee, and Georgia are usually mentioned close to the top. When home biscuit makers talk about their own baking methods, they passionately discuss differences in types of flour, butter temperatures, and heights of the rise. Everyone can't possibly be right.

This biscuit recipe is basic but, when done correctly, will yield pillowy, light, butter biscuits that need nothing more than jam, sausage gravy, or, in the best-case scenario, fried chicken.

6 cups flour, preferably cake flour
¼ cup baking powder
2 tablespoons granulated sugar
1 tablespoon kosher salt
¾ cup (1½ sticks) butter, frozen and grated with a micro plane or box grater
3 cups cold buttermilk

Preheat the oven to 425°F. In a large bowl, whisk together the flour, baking powder, sugar, and salt. Fold in the butter.

Make a well in the middle of the flour and butter mixture. Pour the buttermilk into the well. Use a rubber spatula or wooden spoon to fold together the buttermilk and flour mixture until it forms a shaggy dough. Don't overwork. At this point you want the dough to have some crumbly and some wet spots.

Pour the dough out onto a floured work surface. Flour your hands and bring the dough together by hand. Use additional flour if necessary to keep from sticking. Using your hands or a floured rolling pin, roll and flatten the dough until it's a ¾-inch thick rectangle. To make biscuit layers, fold one side into the center and then the other side. Turn the dough 90 degrees and flatten it to ¾ of an inch again. Repeat the folding step two more times, always returning the dough to ¾ of an inch before repeating. Flatten into a final ¾-inch rectangle.

Using a biscuit cutter, press straight down to cut the dough. Do not turn the biscuit cutter as you cut, or you will prevent a good rise. Continue to rework scraps of dough until you have 12 uniform biscuits.

Arrange biscuits in a cast-iron skillet or on a parchment-lined baking sheet, and bake until golden brown, 20–25 minutes. Serve hot.

OLD-FASHIONED PEACH ICE CREAM

MATT KONIGSMARK | MAKES 2½ QUARTS

Peaches were first cultivated in eastern China. They were introduced to islands off the Georgia coast by Franciscan monks in 1571. The Cherokees in the area began to plant them, and thanks to the mild climate, they grew beautifully. By the time English colonizers arrived, the crop was well established. Georgia's reputation as the "Peach State" was cemented by Raphael Moses, a Confederate officer and planter who was the first to successfully ship peaches to the North, a feat he accomplished by transporting the soft fruit in baskets.

This was the recipe my grandmother Mimi made each summer when the Georgia peaches were ripe.

1 quart fresh peaches, peeled and sliced
3 cups granulated sugar
4 large eggs, beaten
1 (12-ounce) can evaporated milk, chilled
1 cup cold heavy whipping cream
1 quart cold whole milk

In a blender, in batches, puree together portions of the peaches, sugar, eggs, evaporated milk, and whipping cream. Place puree in a bowl. Add whole milk and stir well. Pour the mixture into a 1-gallon ice cream maker and freeze according to manufacturer's directions.

WHITE PEACH BELLINI

THE MUSEUM OF THE AMERICAN COCKTAIL

MAKES 1 COCKTAIL

This drink was invented in 1945 by Giuseppe Cipriani, founder of Harry's Bar in Venice, Italy. The drink received its name in 1948, when a major retrospective exhibition of the Renaissance artist Giovanni Bellini was held in Venice.

You can buy peach puree commercially. To make your own, puree fresh, ripe, peeled peaches.

Ice cubes
2 ounces white peach puree
4 ounces chilled Prosecco

Fill a large mixing glass with ice. Pour in the peach puree, and then gently add the Prosecco. With a bar spoon, carefully stir by dragging the puree up from the bottom, much like folding egg whites. Strain into a champagne flute.

MASTER'S TRANSFUSION

BRENT ROSEN | MAKES 1 COCKTAIL

The origins of the Transfusion cocktail are hazy. Some say Dwight Eisenhower had something to do with it after stepping down from the presidency. Others point toward Augusta National and drinking traditions around the Masters golf tournament. The Transfusion is certainly associated with golf, because the drink is nearly ubiquitous on golf courses and unknown almost everywhere else. But the drink should not be limited to golfers and the golf-adjacent: the Transfusion is just as refreshing on your porch as it is on the fairway. Better still, the Transfusion's ingredients are mainly pantry staples: vodka, grape juice, lime, and ginger ale, making it simple to pull together. When you've switched from whiskey to vodka for the summer, don't forget about the Transfusion, a cocktail for the ages!

Ice cubes
2 ounces vodka
1 ounce Concord grape juice
Juice from 2 lime wedges
4 ounces ginger ale
For serving: lime wedge

Fill a tall glass with ice. Stir in vodka, grape juice, and lime juice. Don't be tempted to add more grape juice; doing so will make the drink too sweet. Top with ginger ale and garnish with a lime wedge.

A still, the power of distilling, and the untold story, in the Kentucky exhibit.

KENTUCKY

KENTUCKY HAS TOUCHED THE ENTIRE WORLD with its food and drinks. One example is its famous son, Harland "Colonel" Sanders, who started a small fried chicken franchise at a gas station in Corbin, Kentucky, long before it became known internationally as KFC. Also world renowned are the mint juleps served at the Kentucky Derby, as well as chocolate and walnut-filled Derby pie. Both are made with Kentucky bourbon, the great American corn whiskey aged in oak-charred barrels.

Kentucky is known for its spreads of garden-fresh vegetables, such as beans, greens, and tomatoes. Its chicken-fried steak, grits, fried okra, fried green tomatoes, and chicken and dumplings all reflect African American roots. Kentucky barbecue is characterized by its use of mutton, as well as pork.

What else hails from Kentucky? Burgoo, from the northwestern region, started out as a hunter's stew made with whatever meats were at hand—squirrel, rabbit, and raccoon, for instance. Although it is always made with peas or beans and okra, today the meat is more often a mixture of chicken and pork, or perhaps game birds. Hot Brown, an open-faced turkey and bacon sandwich covered in Mornay sauce and baked until brown, hails from Louisville. Beer and sausages still reflect the German heritage around Louisville, and several forms of chili are popular throughout the state. Ham biscuits, cakes, and pies round out the state's cuisine.

Perhaps the most famous product that hails from Kentucky is bourbon. The fertile fields of Kentucky make it a natural home for bourbon, which is based on corn, as opposed to spirits made with rye that grows in more northern climates. The Code of Federal Regulations now requires that bourbon be made with a mash consisting of at least 51 percent corn. Kentucky's water also contributes to bourbon's taste. The state rests on deposits of limestone that filter and purify the region's water. These combined factors give us America's unique spirit.

HOT BROWN

ELIZABETH M. WILLIAMS | MAKES 2 OPEN-FACED SANDWICHES

The Hot Brown is a signature sandwich that was invented at Louisville's Brown Hotel shortly after it opened in 1923. The hotel's chefs created the sandwich as an alternative to ham-and-egg late-night suppers for hungry dance patrons. The original version was a hot, open-faced turkey sandwich topped with bacon and a delicate Mornay sauce. The Brown Hotel's perfected recipe adds Pecorino Romano cheese, tomato, and garnishes of paprika and parsley. During Kentucky Derby weekend, more than 14,000 Hot Brown sandwiches are served to Louisville visitors.

SAUCE

2 tablespoons butter
2 tablespoons all-purpose flour
1 cup milk
1 cup half-and-half
½ cup grated Pecorino Romano cheese
Pinch of grated nutmeg

Preheat the oven to 325°F. Melt butter in a saucepan, stir in the flour, and cook 2 minutes, stirring constantly. Stir in the milk and the half-and-half. Bring to a simmer, stirring constantly. As the mixture begins to thicken, remove from heat. Quickly stir in the cheese until it is completely melted. Add the nutmeg and stir. Set aside while you assemble the sandwiches.

THE SANDWICHES

2 thick slices of a good white bread (it is traditional to remove the crust, but that is optional)
8 ounces sliced turkey
2 Roma tomatoes, sliced
Sauce from preceding recipe
4 slices cooked bacon
For serving: paprika and chopped chives

In a heavily buttered casserole dish, place the 2 pieces of bread side by side. Divide the turkey slices between the 2 pieces of bread and arrange it to fit onto the bread in a pile. Cover the turkey slices with the sliced tomatoes. Pour all the sauce over the 2 sandwiches, and place in the hot oven until the sauce is browning and bubbling, about 20 minutes. Remove from the oven. Place 2 bacon slices on each sandwich. and sprinkle with paprika and chives. Serve hot.

BENEDICTINE SANDWICH

BRENT ROSEN | MAKES 12 LARGE OR 24 SMALL FINGER SANDWICHES

When it's teatime in Kentucky, it's time for cucumber-based Benedictine sandwiches. The sandwich has nothing to do with cordials or monks, but instead is named after Jennie Benedict, a revered Louisville cook and hostess. Benedict lived from 1860 until 1928, and her recipes were collected in the *Blue Ribbon Cook Book* (1904). The Benedictine sandwich traditionally features cream cheese, cucumber, onion juice, and hot sauce spread on slices of bread with the crust removed. Modern variations add more components, including bacon, tomato, and lettuce. This version, inspired by the Louisville classic, can be served as a main course. For an afternoon gathering, serve on a platter alongside finger-sized pimento cheese and tomato sandwiches.

8 ounces cream cheese, softened
1 cup peeled, seeded, and chopped cucumber
½ cup finely chopped green onion, both white and green parts
¼ cup chopped fresh dill
2 tablespoons mayonnaise
Heavy dash hot sauce
Salt and pepper, to taste
6 slices white bread

Mix the first 6 ingredients together. Taste and add salt and pepper. If you prefer a spicier spread, add more hot sauce.

Remove crust from bread and spread 4 slices with Benedictine filling. Top sandwiches with remaining bread slices. Cut each sandwich into 3 finger-sized sandwiches.

FRIED CHICKEN

MADDIE HAYES | MAKES 6–8 PIECES

In 1930, in front of a small gas station in Corbin, Kentucky, Harland David Sanders opened Sanders Court and Café, which became the birthplace of Kentucky Fried Chicken. In 1936, Kentucky governor Ruby Laffoon recognized Harland Sanders for his outstanding culinary contributions to the state by bestowing on him the honorary title of "Colonel." In the late 1930s as Sanders's establishment continued to grow, he introduced the famous KFC pressure cooker, a new way to fry fresh chicken faster. By 1952, Colonel Sanders was actively franchising his fried chicken business. The original restaurant closed in 1955, when a new highway caused patrons to bypass the location. Nonetheless, by 1960 there were four hundred franchise units across the United States and Canada. Today Colonel Sanders and Kentucky Fried Chicken (or KFC) are known throughout the world. The American icon wearing a traditional southern white suit is even a common sight in China.

In 1968, after Colonel Sanders sold Kentucky Fried Chicken, he and his wife Claudia embarked on a new culinary venture. They used their restaurant expertise and inventory of delicious southern recipes to open Claudia Sanders Dinner House, which still maintains an old-fashioned family-style service and southern cuisine. Colonel Sanders died in 1980 at the age of eighty.

½ gallon canola, peanut, or vegetable oil for frying
4 cups all-purpose flour
2 tablespoons black pepper
1½ tablespoons salt
1 tablespoon garlic powder
2 teaspoons onion powder
1 teaspoon cayenne pepper
½ cup buttermilk
1 large egg
2 pounds boneless, skinless chicken thighs (preferably), or breasts

Place enough oil to fill a deep cast-iron skillet or Dutch oven with a 1-inch clearance at the top. Reserve the rest of the oil to replace the oil that leaves the skillet with the chicken. Heat the oil to 325°F. In a large bowl, mix together the flour, black pepper, salt, garlic powder, onion powder, and cayenne pepper and set aside.

In a medium bowl, mix together the buttermilk and egg. On your countertop, place the raw chicken farthest away from the frying oil. Next, place the buttermilk mixture and then, closest to the pot, the dry mixture.

Take a piece of chicken and dip it into the buttermilk; then dredge it in the dry mixture, making sure the chicken is evenly coated. Gently lay it in the hot oil. Do not overcrowd the pieces and keep an eye on the oil temperature. Fry chicken until golden brown. The internal temperature should register 165°F on a thermometer.

CORN PUDDING

MIKIE HAYES | MAKES 8 SERVINGS

1 pound bacon
1 medium yellow or sweet onion, chopped
3 tablespoons all-purpose flour
2 teaspoons baking powder
¾ teaspoon salt
½ teaspoon black pepper
1 cup heavy whipping cream
1 cup ricotta cheese
4 large eggs
¼ cup (½ stick) butter, melted
1 tablespoon sugar
3 cups corn kernels, fresh off the cob, frozen and thawed, or drained sweet, canned corn
¾ cup (about 6 ounces) grated cheddar (I like extra-sharp), plus a handful extra to sprinkle on top
For serving: chopped fresh basil

Preheat the oven to 350°F. Grease a 9×13-inch baking dish and set aside. Cook the bacon in the oven on a sheet pan until it's starting to crisp but not to the point that it easily crumbles, about 10 minutes. Leave 3 bacon pieces in the oven and cook them until crisp, about 10 more minutes. Crumble the 3 crispy slices and set aside separately. Reserve 1 tablespoon bacon grease.

In a skillet over medium-high heat, add the tablespoon bacon grease and sauté the chopped onion until translucent, about 5 minutes. In a medium bowl, combine the flour, baking powder, salt, and pepper. In a large bowl, whisk together the cream, ricotta, eggs, butter, and sugar. Gradually add the flour mixture into the cream mixture, whisking until smooth. Stir in corn, onions, and ¾ cup cheddar cheese.

Pour mixture into the prepared baking dish, and top with the partially cooked bacon slices and the extra cheese. Bake until pudding is set and deep golden brown, about 30 minutes. Sprinkle with the reserved bacon crumbles and let cool 5 minutes. Garnish with chopped basil. Serve warm.

BOURBON BALLS

ELIZABETH M. WILLIAMS | MAKES 12

This recipe is a great way to use up stale cookies. If your ginger snaps have lost their snap, this is the recipe for you. You can substitute chocolate wafers or any other kind of hard cookie. For a zestier coating, add chili powder. Substituting coconut or almond flour for the confectioner's sugar will make a less sweet version.

COOKIES

1 cup crumbled ginger snaps
1 cup chopped pecans
1 cup confectioner's sugar
2 tablespoons unsweetened cocoa powder
¼ cup bourbon

COATINGS

½ cup unsweetened cocoa powder
½ cup confectioner's sugar
½ cup ground nuts

To make cookies, stir together the dry ingredients. Thoroughly mix in the bourbon. Cover and refrigerate 2 hours. Remove the dough from the refrigerator. Wet a kitchen towel that you can use to dampen your hands. Roll 2 tablespoons dough into a ball. Wipe your hands on the towel as needed and make balls with all the dough. Set the balls on a tray or plate and keep covered.

To coat the cookie balls, place each of the 3 coatings in separate bowls. Roll the finished cookie balls in one of the coatings. Place each ball in a ruffled cupcake cup. Store in an airtight container up to a week. Just before serving the stored balls, roll them again in the same coating.

BOURBON BANANA PUDDING

MADDIE HAYES | MAKES 6 SERVINGS (MAKE UP TO 5 DAYS AHEAD)

This recipe is best made at least a day ahead, so that the Nilla wafers can soften and soak up that delicious banana flavor.

½ cup granulated sugar
3 tablespoons cornstarch
¼ teaspoon salt
2 cups half-and-half
4 egg yolks
¼ cup (½ stick) salted butter
¼ cup bourbon (optional)
2 teaspoons vanilla extract or vanilla bean paste
2 ripe bananas, mashed, plus 2 bananas, sliced
5 cups Nilla wafers
1 cup Whipped Cream (recipe follows)
For serving: whipped cream, banana slices, crushed Nilla wafers, and peanuts

In a medium saucepan, whisk together the sugar, cornstarch, and salt. Add the half-and-half and egg yolks and stir to combine. Cook over medium heat, whisking constantly, being careful not to scorch the milk or scramble the eggs, until thickened and pudding-like, 10 to 12 minutes. Remove from heat and stir in the butter, bourbon, and vanilla extract. Once cooled, stir in mashed bananas.

In a glass trifle dish, spread the cooled banana pudding with the sliced banana. Top with Nilla wafers and whipped cream. To serve, top each serving with whipped cream, more banana slices, crushed Nilla wafers, and even peanuts, if desired.

WHIPPED CREAM

MAKES 2 CUPS

1 cup heavy whipping cream
2 tablespoons powdered sugar
½ teaspoon vanilla extract or vanilla bean paste

Add all ingredients to a large mixing bowl or a stand mixer, and whip on medium speed until soft peaks form, about 2 to 3 minutes.

OLD FASHIONED

THE MUSEUM OF THE AMERICAN COCKTAIL

MAKES 1 COCKTAIL

It is often claimed that this cocktail was created by Colonel James E. Pepper, a bourbon distiller and a bartender at the Pendennis Club in Louisville. It is more likely that the name "Old Fashioned" was applied to what otherwise would have been known simply as a "whiskey cocktail."

It is common to muddle a half-orange wheel with this drink. Better yet, muddle a slice of orange peel so that you get the trapped essential oils but none of the pulp.

1 sugar cube (1 teaspoon)
1 teaspoon water
2 dashes Angostura bitters
Ice cubes
2 ounces bourbon whiskey
For serving: lemon peel twist or orange slice and cherry

In a rocks glass, muddle together sugar, water, and bitters until the sugar is mostly dissolved. Fill the glass with ice, and then stir in the whiskey. Garnish with a twist of lemon peel or an orange slice and cherry. Serve with a swizzle stick, straw, or both.

THAT'S MY JAM JULEP

LAURA BELLUCCI | MAKES 1 COCKTAIL

The mint julep was the king of early American drinks, not just because it was as powerful as it was delicious, but also because it was the first cocktail to catch on. Along with the Ice Punch, it was also the first to demand the use of ice. SoFAB's version of the julep uses plenty of mint, shaved ice, and whiskey. For additional flavor, we add seasonal Jamboree Jams, products made by Sara Levasseur, a friend of SoFAB. At the time of this writing, we're enjoying our julep with blueberry preserves. If you can't get your hands on Jamboree Jams, any good locally made jam will do.

10 fresh mint leaves, plus a few for garnish
1 teaspoon or bar spoon local, fresh jam
2 ounces bourbon whiskey
Crushed ice

Add the 10 mint leaves and jam to an empty rocks glass. Muddle gently. Add whiskey and stir. Add ice. Roll into a shaker tin and pour back into the rocks glass. Twist the mint garnish between your fingers and top the drink with it.

Red beans and other favorite legumes in the Louisiana exhibit.

LOUISIANA

LOUISIANA'S RESIDENTS—first the Native Americans, then the French and Spanish and those who arrived from Africa under the duress of slavery, and later those who came with dreams of a bright future—all had to begin with ingredients they found around them to survive.

Some tried to ignore what the land told them was possible. The Germans, for example, insisted on cultivating potatoes in the swamp. The French waited on the docks of the Mississippi River for moldy French wheat flour, rather than make do without their precious *gigot de pain*. Yet most people took a laissez-faire attitude to the absence of their favorite foods and accepted their new cuisine in this new country.

Traditional Louisianan cooking is found in three geographical culinary areas. In the traditionally Protestant northern part of the state are found ham, cornbread, chess pie, and fried catfish. The predominantly Catholic southern part of the state cultivated a resourceful savoir faire, not merely making do with the odd ingredients at hand but using them in spectacular dishes that visitors and locals still delight in today. Smoked meats, boudin, and crawfish are specialties in the Cajun parishes in the southwest. The Creole city of New Orleans is known for po'boys, red beans and rice, and the relatively refined dessert Bananas Foster. Both the Cajun and Creole cultures have their own versions of gumbo and jambalaya.

Around the turn of the twentieth century, tens of thousands of Sicilians settled in New Orleans, adding another dimension to the area's food. These immigrants mostly lived in the French Quarter when they first arrived, opening businesses there, including what became known as macaroni factories. These factories used extruders to make dried pasta, introducing the city to this dish and its accompanying tomato sauce. In New Orleans that sauce has come to be called "red gravy." The Sicilians also brought the muffuletta, the meatball po'boy, the Italian sausage po'boy, and snoballs. Today the city stuffs its vegetables with breadcrumbs, not the usual southern staple of rice, thanks to the Sicilians.

Louisiana has robust rice and sugar industries. The state is the nation's second-largest seafood supplier and leads in crawfish production.

Because SoFAB is in Louisiana, we included a few more recipes here than are found in other chapters.

SAVORY CALAS & SWEET CALAS

POPPY TOOKER

Calas are fried rice fritters that at one time were sold by street vendors in New Orleans. In January 2022, we demonstrated savory calas for one of the museum's digital cooking classes, and they were a great hit. The key step is forming calas batter into an oval shape called a "quenelle." Using two spoons, scoop a bit of the mixture, and pass it back and forth between the spoons until you've created a quenelle ball. Drop the balls into the fry oil and watch them bob around until brown.

SAVORY CALAS

MAKES ABOUT 14

Vegetable oil for frying
2 cups cooked rice
½ cup all-purpose flour
2 teaspoons baking powder
¼ teaspoon salt
2 large eggs
4 tablespoons chopped boiled shrimp, plus more for garnish
3 thinly sliced green onions, plus more for garnish
1 tablespoon hot sauce
For serving: your favorite savory dipping sauce

Heat 2 inches oil in a deep fryer or pot to 360°F. Meanwhile, mix together the rice, flour, baking powder, and salt. Thoroughly mix in the eggs, shrimp, green onions, and hot sauce. Use 2 tablespoons to form oval-shaped quenelles and drop the batter into the hot oil. Fry until brown all over, about 4–6 minutes. Drain on paper towels. Garnish with the additional sliced green onions and chopped shrimp. Serve hot with a sauce for dipping.

SWEET CALAS

MAKES ABOUT 12

Vegetable oil for frying
2 cups cooked rice
6 tablespoons all-purpose flour
3 heaping tablespoons sugar
2 teaspoons baking powder
¼ teaspoon salt
2 large eggs
¼ teaspoon vanilla extract
Confectioners' sugar

Heat 2 inches oil in a fryer or deep pot to 360°F. Meanwhile, in a bowl, combine rice, flour, sugar, baking powder, and salt. Mix until rice is coated with the dry ingredients. Add eggs and vanilla and mix well. Using a tablespoon, carefully drop the rice mixture into hot oil and fry until brown all over, 4–6 minutes. Remove from oil with a slotted spoon and drain on paper towels. Sprinkle calas with confectioners' sugar. Serve hot.

CHARGRILLED OYSTERS

BRENT ROSEN | MAKES 24

There is plenty of evidence to support the Indigenous population as the inventors of broiled oysters. They placed oysters into hot coals until the steam inside forced the shells to pop open. This cooking technique made oysters a lot easier to open and eat.

This oyster recipe is nothing more than butter-poached oysters on the half shell. It is inspired by the great chargrilled oyster houses of New Orleans, including Drago's Restaurant, which is credited with popularizing the modern chargrilled oyster. The garlicky, Worcestershire-heavy butter sauce will remind you of the flavors of New Orleans–style barbecued shrimp but with smoky notes. If you don't have a grill, you can use the broiler in your oven. Follow the same directions for grilling but leave the oysters under the broiler a minute or so after you add the cheese.

2 cups grated Parmesan cheese
1 cup grated mozzarella cheese
2 lemons, zested and juiced, plus 1 cup freshly squeezed lemon juice
1 bunch Italian parsley, chopped
1 cup (2 sticks) butter, softened
½ cup Worcestershire sauce
¼ cup Tabasco-brand sriracha sauce
¼ cup minced garlic
1 tablespoon dried oregano
24 large oysters, shucked on the half shell
For serving: hot, crusty bread

Heat a charcoal or gas grill to high heat (maintain a temperature of at least 450°F). Mix together the cheeses, zest and juice from 2 lemons, and chopped parsley. Set aside.

In a small saucepan, melt the butter. Mix the melted butter with the 1 cup lemon juice, Worcestershire sauce, sriracha sauce, garlic, and dried oregano.

Place the oysters in their half shells on the grill directly over the heat source, oyster side up. Spoon the seasoned-butter mixture over the oysters. Let a little drip over the edges of the shells; you want the butter to overflow and cause the grill to flare. Cook until oysters curl up at their sides, about 5 minutes. Top with the reserved cheese mixture and then remove from the grill. Serve hot with bread for dipping.

DIRTY RICE ARANCINI

NINA COMPTON | MAKES 35 APPETIZER SERVINGS

3 tablespoons vegetable oil, divided
1 pound chicken livers, chopped fine in a food processor
½ pound pork sausage
1 cup finely chopped yellow onion, plus 1 medium onion, minced
¾ cup finely chopped green bell pepper
¼ cup finely chopped celery
2 teaspoons minced garlic
1 habanero pepper, minced
1 teaspoon salt
1 tablespoon onion powder
1 tablespoon chopped fresh oregano
1 tablespoon chopped fresh thyme, plus 1 sprig
1 teaspoon ground black pepper
1 teaspoon cayenne pepper
1 pinch chili flakes
⅛ teaspoon paprika
6 cups chicken stock, divided
2 bay leaves
¼ cup (½ stick) butter
3 cups raw Arborio rice
2 cups Parmesan cheese, grated
1 ounce fontina, cut into small pieces
¼ cup fresh minced parsley
3 cups flour, seasoned with salt and pepper
8 large eggs
3 cups panko breadcrumbs, finely ground in a food processor
Vegetable oil for frying
For serving: Sour Orange Mojo (recipe follows)

In a large heavy sauté pan, heat 2 tablespoons of the oil over medium-high heat. Add the chicken livers and sausage and cook, stirring, until the meat is browned, about 6 minutes. Add the remaining tablespoon of oil, the onion, bell pepper, celery, garlic, habanero, salt, onion powder, oregano, 1 tablespoon thyme, black pepper, cayenne, chili flakes, and paprika. Cook, stirring, for 5 minutes. Add ½ cup of the stock and the bay leaves. Scrape the bottom of the pan to loosen any browned bits. Bring to a simmer; then lower the heat and simmer 5 minutes. Remove the bay leaves and set the sausage mixture aside.

To make the rice, in a separate pot, melt the butter and add the minced medium onion. Cook on low heat until the onion is tender, about 5 minutes. Add the rice and cook until the grains are toasted, about 2 minutes. Add the remaining 5½ cups stock in thirds, stirring constantly between additions, until the liquid is absorbed and the rice is tender.

In a large bowl, combine the cooked rice with the sausage mixture. Add the Parmesan cheese and let cool. Mix in the diced fontina. Stir in the parsley and roll into 1½-ounce balls.

Heat 4 inches oil in a deep fryer or large pot to 350°F. Meanwhile, place the seasoned flour in a bowl. Beat the eggs in another bowl. Place the panko in a third bowl. Roll each rice ball in the flour, then in the egg wash, and then in the panko, coating thoroughly. Fry until golden brown, about 4 minutes. Do not crowd.

SOUR ORANGE MOJO

THE MUSEUM OF THE AMERICAN COCKTAIL

MAKES ABOUT 1½ CUPS

6 cloves garlic, finely chopped
1 Scotch bonnet chili, stemmed, seeded, and minced
2 teaspoons whole cumin seeds, freshly toasted
½ teaspoon kosher salt
1 cup pure olive oil
⅓ cup sour orange juice (you can substitute a combo of orange and lime juices)
2 teaspoons Spanish sherry vinegar
Freshly toasted and ground black pepper, to taste

In a mortar, mash together the garlic, Scotch bonnet, cumin, and salt until fairly smooth. Scrape into a medium bowl and set aside. The chili pepper is hot, so do not touch your eyes. Over medium heat, heat the oil in a saucepan until just hot, and pour it over the garlic-chili mix. Stir and then let it stand 10 minutes. Stir in the orange juice, vinegar, and black pepper. Keeps in the refrigerator 2 weeks.

CRAWFISH ÉTOUFFÉE

CAMILLE STAUB & COLLEEN ALLERTON-HOLLIER

MAKES 6 SERVINGS

1 cup (2 sticks) unsalted butter
½ cup all-purpose flour
½ cup chopped onion
2 whole tomatoes, chopped
½ cup chopped celery
½ cup chopped green bell pepper
4 large garlic cloves, chopped
4 cups crawfish or seafood stock
2 bay leaves
2 pounds peeled crawfish tails, with the fat
Salt, black pepper, and cayenne pepper, to taste
For serving: hot cooked rice

In a large, heavy-bottomed pot, melt butter over medium heat. Make a roux by adding flour and stirring constantly until the color of chocolate, about 17 minutes (20 minutes if you want a darker roux.). Add onion and cook, stirring constantly until it is soft.

Add the tomatoes and cook until they have broken down, about 15 minutes. Add celery, bell pepper, and garlic and continue to cook until vegetables are soft, about 7 minutes. Pour in the crawfish stock one cup at a time, stirring between additions. Add the bay leaves and simmer 30 minutes.

Season crawfish tails and fat with salt, pepper, and cayenne. Add crawfish to the sauce and simmer 5 minutes. Adjust seasoning and serve hot over rice.

CAJUN BROWN JAMBALAYA

WAYNE JACOB'S SMOKEHOUSE | MAKES 6 SERVINGS

Family-owned Wayne Jacob's Smokehouse in LaPlace makes an excellent Cajun version of Louisiana's famous one-pot rice dish. Creole jambalaya is made with tomato, which is not traditionally found in the Cajun version.

¼ cup canola oil
1 head celery, diced
3 green bell peppers, seeded and diced
1 large onion, diced
2 bunches green onions, chopped
1 tablespoon chopped garlic
1 pound diced pork
1 pound ground pork
2 links smoked sausage, sliced
½ link andouille, quartered and sliced
1 tablespoon black pepper
1 teaspoon cayenne pepper
1 quart chicken stock, divided
1 quart beef stock, divided
4 cups raw rice
3½ cups water

In a large Dutch oven, heat canola oil and sauté celery, bell peppers, onion, green onions, and garlic until translucent and starting to brown, about 7 minutes. Add all meats, black pepper, and cayenne. Cook until meat is well browned, about 10 minutes, stirring often to prevent sticking. Add 2 cups chicken stock and 2 cups beef stock and deglaze the pot, stirring up the browned bits. Cook, uncovered, until most of the liquid has cooked out, about 40 minutes. Do not let the pan get dry.

Add the remaining 2 cups chicken stock and 2 cups beef stock and simmer 30 minutes. Check for seasoning. It should be strong to account for the addition of rice and water. Add rice and water and stir to make sure the rice doesn't stick to the bottom of the pot. The liquid should be just covering all the ingredients. Bring to a simmer, cover the pot, and reduce heat to low. Cook, covered, for 20 minutes. Turn the fire off and do not open the pot for another 10 minutes. This will ensure that any uncooked rice will be tender. Remove the lid, stir, and serve.

FRIED OYSTER PO'BOY

CHRISTOPHER BLAKE | MAKES 1 LARGE SANDWICH

1 dozen large raw oysters
1 package commercial fish fry mix or 1 cup seasoned flour
Cooking oil for frying
1 (12-inch) section of New Orleans po'boy bread or an equivalent French bread
Soft butter for spreading on bread
Mayonnaise
Enough shredded lettuce to line bread
6–7 thin slices tomato
Pickle slices
Salt
Red pepper sauce
Ketchup
Half a fresh lemon

Drain oysters well. Dredge oysters in fish fry mix and refrigerate.

When ready to make the sandwich, heat 4 inches oil in a skillet or deep fryer to 325°F and also heat the oven to 325°F. Dip the coated oysters once again in the fish fry mix. Drop the oysters in the hot oil one at a time. Do not put them in all at once, and do not overcrowd them. If the skillet is too small, make two batches. When the oysters float to the top, after about 3–4 minutes, they should be golden brown and crisp and can be drained on paper towels.

Split the bread loaf lengthwise and spread the 2 cut sides with butter. Place the bread, buttered side up, in the heated oven for 3 minutes. Remove from the oven and spread the insides with mayonnaise. Layer on lettuce, tomato, pickles, and oysters. Sprinkle oysters with salt and dashes of red pepper sauce. Add ketchup and squeeze lemon juice onto each sandwich. Close the sandwich and serve.

RED BEANS & RICE

VINCE HAYWARD | MAKES 6–8 SERVINGS

Red beans and rice is an iconic food of New Orleans. The humble dish is generally served on Mondays. Lore has it that this tradition began as a way of utilizing the ham bone from Sunday dinner. Because Monday was wash day, a homemaker's duties would focus on her laundry, and she could not stand at a stove all day; hence, her choice of a recipe that practically cooked itself. The boiling pot of beans also conserved fuel by allowing the same fire to be used to cook and to boil the dirty clothes. This dish is such a part of New Orleans that Louis Armstrong used to sign his letters "Red Beans and Rice-ly Yours."

Beans have always had a strong presence in Louisianans' diets. Long before the arrival of Europeans, Native Americans were cultivating a variety of beans, including runner beans, lima beans, and red beans. Their "three sisters" crops—beans, corn, and squash—supplied a nutritionally complete diet. When Europeans arrived, they brought their own history of bean consumption, eating garbanzos, lentils, and other legumes.

Bean preparation can be forgiving to a cook who must tend to other duties. Bean dishes are also a way of stretching a small quantity of meat to feed a large number of people. These two qualities made them very appealing to cooks across the state. Italians, Alsatian Germans, Cajuns, and Spaniards all ate beans in their countries of origin, and they brought a variety of methods of preparing them to Louisiana. Creole recipes often call for ham or pickled pork as seasoning meat, while Cajun recipes call for andouille sausage or tasso, reflective of local tastes.

As to red beans' popularity with home cooks, one can look at their presence in cookbooks to ascertain their prevalence. It is worth noting that Lafcadio Hearn's *Creole Cook Book* (1885), a book that aimed to present "a number of recipes . . . embracing the entire field of La Cuisine Creole," contains only four bean recipes, and none of them for red beans. However, *The Picayune Creole Cookbook* (1901) contains seven recipes for red beans alone in a listing of eighteen bean recipes. This may imply that bean consumption rose in those sixteen years, or perhaps Lafcadio Hearn was not a bean fan. Regardless, the recipe for red beans and rice from 1901 would be recognized by any home cook today, although there is no mention of it allowing the cook to tend to washing and not the bean pot.

1 pound Camellia Brand dried red kidney beans
1 pound smoked sausage, sliced
2 tablespoons butter
2 cups blend of chopped seasoning vegetables (onion, celery, green bell peppers, parsley), purchased or homemade
1 clove garlic, minced
10 cups water
1 bay leaf
2 smoked ham hocks
Salt, pepper, and Cajun seasoning, to taste
3 dashes hot sauce
For serving: hot cooked white rice

Rinse and sort beans. In a large heavy pot set over medium-high heat, sauté sliced sausage 5 minutes. Add butter and then the seasoning vegetables and garlic. Cook, stirring occasionally, until onion turns soft and clear, about 8 to 10 minutes. Stir in beans, water, and the bay leaf. Add the ham hocks. Bring to a rolling boil and cook uncovered for 30 minutes, stirring every 10 minutes. Reduce heat and simmer covered until beans are tender, 1–2 hours, stirring occasionally. As beans soften, use a large spoon to mash a portion against the side of the pot to create a thick gravy.

When the beans are done, add salt, pepper, and Cajun seasoning to taste. Add hot sauce and stir well. Serve over hot cooked rice.

LENA RICHARD'S STUFFED BAKED TOMATOES

ASHLEY ROSE YOUNG | MAKES 6 SERVINGS

Lena Richard was an African American chef who built a culinary empire in New Orleans during the Jim Crow era. She reshaped the public's understanding of New Orleans's cuisine by showcasing and celebrating the Black roots of Creole cooking at a time when racial stereotypes pervaded the food industry. In the racially segregated South, Richard owned and operated catering businesses, eateries, a fine-dining restaurant, a cooking school, and an international frozen food business. Her reputation as one of New Orleans's finest chefs launched her into early food TV at a time when there were few African American stars.

Lena Richard's Cook Book, published in 1939, was the first cookbook by an African American featuring New Orleans Creole cuisine. A year later, Houghton Mifflin published the book for a broader national audience under a different title, *New Orleans Cook Book.* The recipe below is adapted from Richard's recipe for stuffed baked tomatoes. The cooking process slowly unveils the natural sweetness of the heirloom tomatoes, slightly caramelizing their sugars; the tomatoes pair beautifully with the shrimp filling.

10 shrimp, peeled (or about enough for ½ cup after being cooked and chopped)
2 teaspoons olive oil
Salt and pepper, to taste
1 tablespoon freshly squeezed lemon juice
6 medium-sized tomatoes
2 tablespoons finely chopped celery
1 tablespoon chopped onion
4 tablespoons (½ stick) melted butter, divided
½ cup soft breadcrumbs, divided

Preheat the oven to 350°F. Gently dry the shrimp with a paper towel. Heat olive oil in a skillet over medium heat. Sauté shrimp for 3 minutes on each side. Season with salt and pepper. Remove from heat and add the lemon juice, swirling the sauté pan so that the juice coats all the shrimp. Place shrimp in a bowl and set aside. Once cool, chop the shrimp.

To prepare the tomatoes, cut a slice from the stem end of each tomato and scoop out the center and put it in a bowl. Mix together the tomato pulp, celery, and onion. Strain the vegetable mixture. Set aside the juices for another use or discard. To the strained vegetables, add 2 tablespoons melted butter, ¾ of the breadcrumbs, and the chopped shrimp. Fold the mixture together.

Lightly salt and pepper the insides of the tomatoes. Stuff with the vegetable and shrimp mixture. Top each stuffed tomato with the remainder of the dry breadcrumbs and a small pat of butter.

Lightly butter a large oven-proof skillet. Place stuffed tomatoes in it and bake for a total of 45 minutes, moving the skillet to the top rack of the oven for the last 20 minutes so that the breadcrumbs brown and the tomato skins pucker slightly at the edges. Remove from the oven and serve.

GUMBO

POPPY TOOKER | MAKES 10–12 SERVINGS

If one dish can represent a culture, in Louisiana that dish most certainly is gumbo. It is the *sine qua non,* something indispensable, of our cuisine and the DNA of the people of south Louisiana. Like DNA, everyone's gumbo is different. But we recognize it all as gumbo.

From the point of view of an outsider, the word "gumbo" evokes the geographic area and its sense of place, the people and our attitudes, a savory soup, a wonderful flavor, a mélange (often a strange one), and a sense of welcome and comfort.

For the insider, gumbo means family, identity, and comfort. We learn about each other by tasting each other's gumbo. While each of us thinks that our gumbo is definitive, we also recognize location, season, and personality from the gumbo of others. The sharing of gumbo has its own traditions and customs, mixing religion, play, and social status.

The making of gumbo is its own ritual. Whether you start from land or sea, catching and growing your own ingredients, or buying them at a farmer's market or store, the pot, the method, the ritual all are sacred. Each gumbo maker has a fat of choice:

lard, bacon fat, olive oil, or duck fat. Likewise, a thickener of choice. Some people prefer okra, that wonderful vegetable that reflects the African contributions to gumbo (in addition to the very name of the dish). Others prefer Native American filé, dried leaves of the sassafras tree, and a rich spice from the New World. Most people also make a roux, reflecting the French contribution to gumbo.

Here is where the heated discussions begin. Can you use all three thickeners? Never! Why not? Should you add tomatoes? If so, only in seafood gumbo? Never in seafood gumbo? Never with okra? Never without okra? You get the idea. People can talk for hours about how thick the gumbo should be and how dark to make the roux. This is a state that really cares about its food. Everyone from every rank and file is willing to voice an opinion. The beauty of this is that everyone else is willing to listen.

2 pounds medium shrimp, peeled, heads and shells reserved
1 onion, chopped, peelings reserved
3 stalks celery, chopped, bottoms and tops reserved
1 bunch green onions, thinly sliced, trimmings reserved
1 pint oysters, with liquor
3 tablespoons vegetable oil
1 cup all-purpose flour
½ cup oil of preference (for roux)
1 bell pepper, chopped
14 cups shrimp stock (see first step)
1 pound gumbo crabs or ½ pound claw crabmeat
1 (1-pound) can crushed tomatoes
2 pounds fresh okra, sliced ¼-inch thick
3 cloves garlic, minced
2 teaspoons dried thyme
2 bay leaves
Salt and ground black pepper
¼ cup Crystal-brand hot sauce
For serving: hot cooked rice

Make a stock in a stock pot by combining shrimp heads and shells, onion peelings, celery bottoms and tops, and green onion trimmings. Cover with 2 inches of water and boil 15 minutes. Strain stock and reserve.

Drain oysters and reserve oyster liquor. Fry okra in a skillet in 3 tablespoons of very hot vegetable oil until lightly browned (or roast). Set aside. In a heavy-bottomed Dutch oven or large pot, make a roux by cooking the flour and ½ cup oil of preference over medium heat, stirring constantly, until it's brown like milk chocolate. Add onions and stir until the roux darkens to a bittersweet chocolate brown.

Add celery and bell pepper and sauté 5 minutes. Add the shrimp stock, oyster liquor, gumbo crabs, tomatoes, okra, garlic, thyme, and bay leaves. Add salt and pepper to taste. Simmer, uncovered, 45 minutes or longer. Ten minutes before serving, add shrimp, green onions, and hot sauce. Bring back to a simmer and cook 10 minutes. Salt as needed. Serve over cooked rice.

NECTAR SNOBALL SYRUP

ELIZABETH M. WILLIAMS | MAKES APPROXIMATELY 3 CUPS

Nectar syrup is a sweet, pink, almond and vanilla flavoring syrup. It was created by pharmacist I. L. Lyons in New Orleans during the late nineteenth century. Lyons sold it to local soda counters, where it quickly became a favorite. After the early 1980s, soda fountains and nectar syrup lost popularity. However, flavored syrups have experienced a revival due to the popularity of snoball stands and ice cream parlors.

This is our family version of the famous New Orleans nectar syrup. You can find it on snoballs, of course, but it is really great in cocktails. Just as Herbsaint and Peychaud's bitters make you think of New Orleans cocktails wherever you are, so can nectar syrup. Try it in any drink instead of grenadine or even instead of simple syrup. It also deliciously moistens pound cake and sweetens fruit salad.

3½ cups granulated sugar
2 cups water
2 tablespoons almond extract
1 tablespoon vanilla extract
¼ cup grenadine syrup

Place the sugar and water in a pot and heat to a simmer. Cook until the sugar is dissolved. Remove from heat and cool to room temperature. Stir in the extracts and grenadine. Place in a bottle and keep in the refrigerator.

Photo courtesy of Brennan's Restaurant.

BANANAS FOSTER

BRENNAN'S RESTAURANT | MAKES 4 SERVINGS

Bananas were not introduced to North America until after the Civil War. Some decades later, when widespread consumption of the fruit took hold, New Orleans became a major center for banana imports from Central and South America.

This iconic dessert was invented by Brennan's Restaurant owner Owen Brennan, the uncle of Ralph Brennan, the third-generation restaurateur and current owner of Brennan's Restaurant. In 1951, Owen asked his sister Ella and Brennan's chef Paul Blangé to come up with a new dessert using bananas and to name it after his friend Richard Foster, then chair of the New Orleans Crime Commission. At the time, Owen's younger brother John (Ralph Brennan's father) was running Brennan's Processed Potato Company, a produce company that had a surplus of bananas. What they came up with is the world-renowned Bananas Foster. The dramatic, flambéed dessert is the most-ordered item on Brennan's menu. Each year, the restaurant sautés 35,000 pounds of bananas tableside in South American rum.

1 cup brown sugar
¼ cup (½ stick) unsalted butter
½ teaspoon ground cinnamon
¼ cup banana liqueur
4 bananas, cut in half lengthwise, then halved
¼ cup dark rum
4 large scoops vanilla ice cream, in individual serving dishes

Combine brown sugar, butter, and cinnamon in a large sauté pan. Place pan over low heat and cook, stirring constantly until the sugar dissolves. Stir in banana liqueur, and then place the bananas in the pan. After the bananas soften and begin to brown, about 2 minutes, carefully add rum. Cook until the rum is hot, and then tip the pan slightly so that it catches your stove flame and ignites the rum. (Or use a match.) When flames subside, place 4 banana slices on top of the ice cream in each dish. Generously spoon on warm sauce and serve immediately.

SoFAB SAZERAC

LAURA BELLUCCI | MAKES 1 COCKTAIL

The Sazerac House first appeared in 1853 on New Orleans's Royal Street, near where the Hotel Monteleone stands today. It was then called Sazerac Coffee House, although the fact that it was named after a popular brandy suggests that coffee was not its most prominent beverage. New Orleanians considered themselves too refined for saloons, so they referred to their tippling establishments as "coffee houses"—of which more than two hundred were listed in the city directory in 1859. Over time, the Sazerac cocktail became the house drink of New Orleans. Even after the 1912 federal ban on absinthe, the party continued with Herbsaint, and nothing much changed in New Orleans.

1 sugar cube
6–8 dashes Peychaud's bitters
2 ounces rye whiskey
Ice cubes
Absinthe or Herbsaint, to rinse
Twist of lemon

Put a sugar cube in the bottom of a pint mixing glass. Saturate with 6–8 healthy dashes of bitters. Muddle the sugar cube until it forms a paste. Add the whiskey and ice and then stir for 30 seconds. Swirl the inside of a chilled old-fashioned glass with the absinthe, discarding any excess. Strain the rye mixture into the glass. Squeeze the lemon peel over the glass to release the oils. Serve immediately.

BRANDY MILK PUNCH

ELIZABETH M. WILLIAMS | MAKES ABOUT 60 (4-OUNCE) SERVINGS

2 quarts whole milk
1 quart heavy cream
4 cups bourbon
2 cups dark rum
½ cup simple syrup or more, to taste
For serving: freshly grated nutmeg

Whisk together the first four ingredients in a large pitcher or punch bowl until well blended. Stir in simple syrup to taste. Chill, covered, at least 1 hour. Serve in individual glasses and top with grated nutmeg, or in a punch bowl sprinkled with nutmeg.

Note: Leftover punch freezes well. When ready to serve, partially thaw and serve as a frozen drink. The alcohol keeps it slushy.

CAFÉ BRÛLOT

BRENT ROSEN | MAKES 10 SERVINGS

Galatoire's might be one of the best old-school dining experiences in the world. It's not so much a restaurant as a private club you get to enjoy for as long as you keep eating and drinking. If you are seated at 11:00 a.m., it's possible to remain until 7:00 or 8:00 p.m. When menus are brought back around after lunch to order dinner, we refer to that as "playing through."

Pimm's Cups, martinis, and wine flow throughout meals of buttery amandine seafood, the world's best Oysters Rockefeller, and remoulade everything. The end of the meal brings another joy: tableside Café Brûlot prepared by Galatoire's many long-time servers. This drink is a mix of cognac, coffee, and various spices and citruses that are flambéed and then poured into coffee. The showmanship is the key—if you're going to pour a flaming drink from a gravy boat, don't be timid about it.

16 lumps sugar (about ⅓ cup)
2¼ jiggers cognac
24 whole cloves
4 sticks cinnamon
4 large twists orange peel
2 twists lemon peel
10 demitasse cups of strong, hot coffee

Light the burner under a brûlot bowl or chafing dish with the flame on low. Put the sugar, cognac, cloves, cinnamon, orange peel, and lemon peel into the bowl. Heat, stirring constantly with a long-handled ladle, until the sugar dissolves and the mixture is warm, about 2 minutes. Remove the orange peel. Ignite the cognac with a match and pour in the hot coffee. While the mixture continues to flame, pour into coffee cups and garnish with the cooked orange peel.

Note: If you play with fire, you may get burned. Be careful when making this punch. Before you do this trick for a crowd, try igniting the cognac a few times.

FRENCH 75

THE MUSEUM OF THE AMERICAN COCKTAIL | MAKES 1 COCKTAIL

With "French" in the name, you might think this drink would use brandy or cognac as the base spirit, but it is properly made with gin. Making its first printed appearance in 1930 in Harry Craddock's *The Savoy Cocktail Book,* this cocktail is named after a 75-millimeter field gun used by French forces and the U.S. National Guard during World War I.

Ice cubes
¾ ounce gin
½ ounce lemon juice
½ ounce simple syrup
4 ounces chilled Champagne

In a shaker, add ice, gin, lemon juice, and simple syrup. Shake well. Strain into a large ice-filled wine glass. Fill with champagne and serve.

HURRICANE

LAURA BELLUCCI | MAKES 1 COCKTAIL

Pat O'Brien's in the New Orleans French Quarter introduced this sweet rum-based drink during World War II when there was a nationwide shortage of whiskey. The drink's name comes from the shape of the glass it's traditionally served in, which resembles a hurricane lamp's glass shade.

Crushed ice
1 ounce white rum
1 ounce gold rum
½ ounce passion fruit puree
1 ounce fassionola syrup
½ ounce lime juice
½ ounce dark rum
For serving: orange slice and a cherry

Fill a tall glass with crushed ice. In a separate glass, mix all ingredients except the dark rum and pour into the ice-filled glass. Float the dark rum on top. Garnish with an orange slice and cherry.

Spotlight from the Maryland exhibit.

MARYLAND

AS IN MOST OTHER SOUTHERN STATES, Maryland's food is influenced by Native American and African traditions. Enslaved Africans, mostly working in tobacco fields, foraged purslane, pokeweed, lamb's quarters (an annual nonwoody plant), and dandelions from ditches, roads, and fields. They planted okra, corn, and peas. Cornmeal ashcakes were seasoned with vinegar, peppers, and whatever greens were at hand. Maryland Woodland tribes grew the three sisters—corn, squash, and beans—and hunted wild fowl, elk, deer, rabbits, and bear. They also ate wild berries and fish from the rivers on their lands.

Today, stuffed ham, fried chicken, and beaten biscuits are waiting for you at the table in Maryland. Potato pie from the Eastern Shore is another specialty, as are Moravian cookies and great popcorn.

Old Bay Seasoning is the aroma of Maryland tables everywhere, because it is used to season Chesapeake Bay oysters, crabs, and fish. The Maryland seafood industry has historically fed the Atlantic coast. As abundant as seafood industries were and are in other parts of the South, Maryland's industry was strategically located to serve not only the state but also the industrial North, especially before refrigeration.

Muskrat is annually trapped in Maryland. Since 1938, muskrat has been celebrated with a national muskrat skinning contest and a cooking contest, with cooking tools that include hand-forged forks and massive cast-iron pots and kettles.

COASTAL CRAB DIP

MIKIE HAYES | MAKES 3½ CUPS

- 1 (16-ounce) container lump or claw crab meat
- 1¼ cups shredded medium cheddar cheese, divided
- 1 (8-ounce) package cream cheese, softened
- ½ cup sour cream
- ¼ cup mayonnaise, preferably Duke's
- 2 teaspoons Worcestershire sauce
- 1½ teaspoons Old Bay seasoning
- 1 teaspoon onion salt
- ½ teaspoon ground mustard
- ½ teaspoon smoked paprika
- 2–4 dashes hot sauce
- 1 teaspoon freshly squeezed lemon juice
- 2 tablespoons chopped scallion greens or chives
- For serving: crostini or crackers like Ritz or club crackers

Preheat the oven to 375°F. Drain the crab well, pick out any pieces of shell, and set aside. In a large bowl, add a cup of the cheddar, the cream cheese, sour cream, mayonnaise, Worcestershire sauce, Old Bay, onion salt, mustard, paprika, and hot sauce. Mix by hand or beat on medium mixer speed until combined.

Gently stir the lemon juice into the crab meat and fold it into the creamed mixture. Try not to break crab pieces up. Transfer to a 2-quart baking pan and sprinkle the remaining ¼ cup cheddar cheese on top. Bake until bubbly around the edges, about 25 minutes. Remove from oven and top with chopped scallion. Serve warm with crostini or crackers.

CRAB CAKE BENEDICT WITH CORN & TOMATO RELISH

BRIGITTE BLEDSOE | MAKES 4 SERVINGS

16 Fried Green Tomatoes (recipe follows)
Corn and Tomato Relish (recipe follows)
16 asparagus spears, cooked to preference
8 Crab Cakes (recipe follows)
8 large eggs
1 cup hollandaise sauce, purchased or homemade
½ cup diced fresh tomatoes
4 teaspoons chopped fresh chives
4 pinches Old Bay seasoning

FRIED GREEN TOMATOES

MAKES 16 SLICES

3 medium-sized green tomatoes
1 cup all-purpose flour
1 cup cornmeal
1 cup granulated sugar
1 tablespoon Cajun seasoning mix
½ cup buttermilk
2½ teaspoons honey
Canola oil for frying

Slice tomatoes about a ¼-inch thick and place in a large bowl. In a separate bowl, combine flour, cornmeal, sugar, and Cajun seasoning. In another bowl, mix buttermilk and honey together and then pour over tomatoes. Gently toss to coat.

Place each green tomato slice into the dry batter and coat well on both sides. Set aside. Pour 3 inches oil into a nonstick skillet and heat to 350°F. Place battered green tomatoes in the hot oil and fry 2 minutes; then flip them over. Cook until golden brown on both sides, about 4 minutes total. Serve alone or with crab cakes.

CORN & TOMATO RELISH

MAKES 2 CUPS

2 ears fresh corn, roasted and kernels cut off
½ red bell pepper, diced small
¼ red onion, diced small
1 garlic clove, minced
2 tablespoons diced fresh tomato
1 tablespoon red wine vinegar
1 tablespoon neutral cooking oil, like canola or peanut oil
1 teaspoon diced fresh jalapeño pepper
1 teaspoon chopped fresh chives
1 teaspoon salt
1 teaspoon pepper
½ teaspoon Tabasco hot sauce
⅛ teaspoon freshly squeezed lemon juice

Combine all ingredients in a bowl. Refrigerate until ready to serve.

CRAB CAKES

MAKES 8

1 cup of your favorite mayonnaise
1 large egg
1 tablespoon yellow mustard
1 teaspoon Worcestershire sauce
¼ teaspoon Old Bay seasoning
1 pinch kosher salt
1 dash Tabasco hot sauce
1 pound jumbo lump crabmeat, picked over for shells
¼ cup diced roasted red peppers
1 tablespoon chopped parsley
¼ cup cracker meal

Preheat the oven to 350°F. In a large bowl, combine mayonnaise, egg, mustard, Worcestershire sauce, Old Bay, salt, and Tabasco. Gently mix in the crabmeat, diced red peppers, and parsley. Gently mix in the cracker meal. Portion into 3-ounce balls and slightly flatten, then place on a nonstick baking sheet. Bake until brown, 20–25 minutes. Serve warm.

Assembly

To assemble, on 4 large serving plates, first place fried green tomato slices on each plate's four corners, for a total of 4 per plate. In the center of each plate, place a scoop of corn and tomato relish. Lay 4 asparagus spears around the relish on each plate. Place one crab cake over 2 fried green tomatoes, opposite each other on the plates, for a total of 2 crab cakes per plate.

Poach the 8 eggs and place one on top of each crab cake. Top each egg with hollandaise sauce, and sprinkle with tomatoes and chives. Sprinkle Old Bay over the entire dish. Serve immediately.

Photo courtesy of Camille Staub.

SHRIMP SALAD & GARLIC AIOLI

CAMILLE STAUB | MAKES 5 POUNDS, SERVING ABOUT 12

This is a good dish for a buffet table.

- 5 pounds boiled shrimp, peeled and finely chopped
- 2 cups Quick Garlic Aioli (recipe follows)
- 1 cup finely diced red onion
- 1 cup finely diced celery
- 1 cup finely diced jalapeño pepper
- ½ cup chopped fresh dill
- ¼ cup chopped fresh chives
- 1 teaspoon sweet paprika
- Zest of 1 lemon
- Juice of 2 lemons
- Salt and pepper, to taste

Place all ingredients in a very large serving bowl and toss. Serve immediately.

QUICK GARLIC AIOLI

MAKES ABOUT 2 CUPS

- 2 cups Duke's mayonnaise
- 10 cloves garlic, peeled
- 2 tablespoons lemon juice
- 1 tablespoon Dijon mustard
- 1 teaspoon Worcestershire sauce
- Salt, to taste

In a food processor or blender, blend ingredients together until smooth.

HUSHPUPPIES WITH HONEY BUTTER & COCKTAIL SAUCE

MIKIE HAYES | MAKES 20–24

1½ cups cornmeal
½ cup all-purpose flour
3 tablespoons sugar
1½ teaspoons baking powder
½ teaspoon garlic powder
½ teaspoon onion powder
2 pinches salt
Pinch or 2 of cayenne pepper
1 cup full-fat buttermilk
1 large egg
Vegetable oil for frying (not olive oil)
For serving: Honey Butter and Cocktail Sauce (recipes follow)

To make hushpuppies, combine the cornmeal, flour, sugar, baking powder, garlic powder, onion powder, salt, and cayenne pepper in a bowl. In a separate bowl, whisk together buttermilk and egg. Stir the buttermilk mixture into the dry mixture just until combined. It's okay if it looks a bit lumpy. Let the batter sit in the refrigerator 20–30 minutes. Don't stir it again.

While the batter chills, heat approximately 3 inches oil to 350°F in a 4- or 5-quart deep cast-iron pot, a heavy-bottomed Dutch oven, or a deep fryer. Once the oil is hot, use a tablespoon or cookie-dough scoop sprayed with cooking spray to carefully drop the batter into the hot oil. Cooking in batches of 6–8, fry, flipping over once, until golden brown, 3–5 minutes. (Test one to make sure it's cooked through.) Drain on paper towels. Between batches, be sure to bring oil back up to 350°F and keep cooked hushpuppies warm in a baking dish in a 200°F oven. Serve them warm with honey butter and cocktail sauce.

HONEY BUTTER

MAKES 1 CUP

1 cup (2 sticks) salted butter, at room temperature

⅓–½ cup local honey, depending on sweetness desired

½ teaspoon cinnamon

Whip ingredients together and serve in a bowl. Refrigerate leftovers.

COCKTAIL SAUCE

MAKES ABOUT 1 CUP

1 cup ketchup

1 tablespoon prepared horseradish

2 teaspoons Worcestershire sauce

2 teaspoons Old Bay Seasoning

2 teaspoons freshly squeezed lemon juice

1 teaspoon granulated garlic

½ teaspoon ground black pepper

Mix all ingredients together in a bowl. Cover and refrigerate.

OLIVE OIL CHOCOLATE CHIP COOKIES

DEE LAVIGNE | MAKES 12 DOZEN COOKIES

1 cup extra virgin olive oil
¾ cup granulated sugar
¾ cup dark brown sugar
1 tablespoon pure vanilla extract
1 teaspoon salt
1 large egg
2 cups all-purpose flour
½ teaspoon baking soda
2 cups semisweet chocolate chips

Preheat your oven to 350°F and line two baking sheets with parchment paper. In a mixing bowl, combine the olive oil, both sugars, vanilla, and salt. Mix on medium-high speed until smooth, about 2 minutes. Add the egg and mix until completely smooth. Add the flour and baking soda and mix just until it's fully incorporated and you don't see any dry spots of flour. Fold in the chocolate chips.

Use your hands to shape the batter into balls, about 2 tablespoons each. Your hands will be greasy from the oil, but for this recipe, I find it is best to use them. As you go, place the dough balls 2 inches apart on the prepared baking sheets. Use the palm of your hand to gently flatten the balls of batter about halfway.

Bake until the cookies are golden brown along the edges, 10–12 minutes. Cool on the baking sheet 5 minutes; then place them on a cooling rack and cool to room temperature.

SMITH ISLAND CAKE

ELIZABETH M. WILLIAMS | MAKES A 9-INCH (8-LAYER) CAKE

This cake is Maryland's official state dessert, likely because it is not only delicious but also represents families sending a bit of themselves with oystermen as they left the island for the harvest. The layers are thin but numerous: sometimes nine to as many as fourteen layers. The frosting is chocolate fudge, which keeps all those layers fresh.

Because the layers are thin, they cool quickly, so make the icing first and let it cool, and then make the cake. That way everything will be ready at about the same time.

ICING

1⅔ cups granulated sugar
1 cup heavy cream
6 tablespoons butter
4 ounces bittersweet chocolate
2 teaspoons corn syrup
1 teaspoon vanilla
¼ teaspoon salt

Place all the ingredients except the vanilla and salt into a heavy-bottomed saucepan. Place over low heat to melt and blend everything. Stir often to ensure that the sugar is fully incorporated and to keep the ingredients from scorching.

Bring the mixture to a boil. Boil one minute and remove from heat. Add the vanilla and the salt and stir. Set aside and allow to cool and thicken. This should take at least an hour. After 2 hours you may need to reheat it to soften it.

CAKE

3¾ cups all-purpose flour
1 teaspoon baking powder
¾ teaspoon baking soda
2 cups granulated sugar
3 sticks butter, at room temperature
5 large eggs, at room temperature
2½ teaspoons vanilla extract
1¾ cups buttermilk, at room temperature

Preheat your oven to 350°F and butter 8 (9-inch) round cake pans (or use as many pans as you have and repeat the baking until you have 8 layers. Do not cook a thick layer and cut it; this makes the cut layers too porous.) Cut parchment rounds to fit the bottoms of the pans, insert them in the pans, and butter them. Flour the insides of the pans completely.

In a large bowl, sift together the flour, baking powder, and baking soda. Set aside. Place the sugar and butter in a mixing bowl and beat for 4 minutes on high speed. Add the eggs, one at a time, beating at least one minute after adding each egg. Add the vanilla with the last egg.

Reduce the mixer speed to low and add ⅓ of the flour mixture, scraping down the sides of the bowl if necessary. Add ⅓ of the buttermilk. Alternate the dry ingredients and the buttermilk 2 more times until just incorporated. Don't overbeat or the cake will be tough.

Place 1 cup of batter in each pan. Bake until a toothpick inserted in the middle comes out dry, about 12 minutes. Remove the pans and cool 2 minutes. Invert the pans onto the counter and carefully remove the parchment while the layers are still warm. If reusing pans, clean and rebutter them, add a new parchment circle, rebutter it, and flour the pan. Add another cup to each pan and repeat until you have used all the batter. You should have 8 layers.

When the layers are cooled, place one layer in the center of a cake stand or plate. Spread a thin layer of the icing on the top. Add another layer and repeat until all the layers are stacked. (Be careful not to spread too much icing between layers, or you might run out.) Ice the outside of the cake, and it's ready to serve.

CARAMEL CORN

JENNIE MERRILL BOUDREAUX | MAKES 5 CUPS

5 cups plain popped popcorn (about ¼ cup kernels)
½ cup (1 stick) salted butter
½ cup light brown sugar, packed
1 tablespoon corn syrup
2 teaspoons salt
1 teaspoon vanilla extract
¼ teaspoon baking soda

Place the popped popcorn in a large bowl and set aside. Lay a 2-foot piece of parchment paper or wax paper on your counter top. In a medium saucepan, combine the butter, brown sugar, and corn syrup over medium heat. Bring to a boil, stirring constantly until the sugar is melted. Boil until mixture begins to thicken, about 3–4 minutes, stirring and scraping the pan regularly.

Remove the pan from the heat and quickly stir in the salt, vanilla, and baking soda. The sugar mixture will bubble and froth. Continue stirring until the sauce becomes thick and glossy.

Slowly pour the sauce over the popcorn. Stir until the popcorn is evenly coated. Pour the popcorn mixture onto the parchment paper. Break up large clumps. Cool and serve. Keeps well in an airtight container at room temperature for up to 3 days.

PAINKILLER

THE MUSEUM OF THE AMERICAN COCKTAIL

MAKES 1 COCKTAIL

The Painkiller cocktail pops up in bars all over Maryland. The original recipe was invented by Daphne Henderson around 1980, although some attribute it to George and Marie Myrick, circa 1971. Either way, it originated at the Soggy Dollar Bar on the island of Jost Van Dyke in the British Virgin Islands. This drink is trademarked by Pusser's and should always be made with Pusser's Navy Rum.

4 ounces fresh pineapple juice
2 ounces Pusser's Rum
1 ounce cream of coconut
1 ounce fresh orange juice
Ice cubes
For serving: freshly grated nutmeg

Shake drink ingredients well with ice and strain into a tall glass filled with ice. Sprinkle the top with freshly grated nutmeg.

THE CAMPARI SUN

BRENT ROSEN | MAKES 12 SERVINGS

Will Abner is the originator of the Campari Sun, which is not really a punch but certainly drinks like one. Describing the alcoholic drink a few years ago, Will said, "The Campari Sun is an easy drinking play on the shandy. The bitter citrus flavors of the grapefruit and Campari are blended away by the beer, leaving nothing but a crisp finish. Served cold, it's a refreshing party beverage that's great to pre-make and keep on ice in the biggest bucket you can find. Three or four of them is the magic number for bocce ball success. Any less, you aren't loose enough. Any more, you are too loose." There's not much else to say about this, other than that it's a perfect beverage for gazing off Maryland's coast.

18 ounces grapefruit juice
6 ounces Campari
12 bottles cold Natty Boh beer (or a beer of your choice)
12 long paper straws

In an easy-pour pitcher, mix the grapefruit juice and Campari together. Pour a few ounces from each bottle of beer into a cup. Top each partially full beer bottle with the grapefruit mixture. Serve each with a paper straw. Alternatively, pour over ice in a glass and serve with a citrus wedge.

GOVERNMENT WARNING: (1) ACCORDING TO
GENERAL, WOMEN SHOULD NOT DRINK
BEVERAGES DURING PREGNANCY BECAUSE
BIRTH DEFECTS. (2) CONSUMPTION
BEVERAGES IMPAIRS YOUR ABILITY TO
OPERATE MACHINERY, AND MAY CAUSE
IMPORTED BY CROWN IMPORTS, CHICAGO
BEER

A corner of the Shed in the Mississippi exhibit.

MISSISSIPPI

FROM CATFISH AND PECANS to honey and chicken, the food of Mississippi is the quintessential food of the South. Agrarian traditions are strong and plentiful in a state rich with important waterways, including the Mississippi River, the Yazoo River Delta, and the Gulf of Mexico. These waters and the fields they cut through have created a diverse culture of foodways.

Reflecting the complex heritage of the Vicksburg delta region, the Delta tamale is made with seasoned meat, traditionally pork, and corn masa. No one is sure who introduced these wildly popular tamales to Mississippi, but they have been a staple since at least the early twentieth century.

Mississippi's Gulf Coast serves up crabs, shrimp, and fish in popular dishes like gumbo, hushpuppies, and fried seafood. All of Mississippi serves up meat and three, a plate lunch with meat or another protein and three sides. Those sides could be macaroni and cheese, potato salad, stewed greens, or black-eyed peas. Just about everyone eats pork in its many forms, from chitlins to ham to pork chops, influenced primarily by enslaved Africans and later by African American cooks and chefs. Cakes like chocolatey, gooey Mississippi Mud Cake are extremely popular. Caramel cake, which takes a simple ingredient like sugar and makes it taste rich and complex, is especially loved.

Mississippians, like others in the South, celebrate and mourn together at the table. Funerals usually wind down with a communal meal. Church picnics and suppers are common, as are extended family celebrations. The hospitality of a shared meal helps explain the fundamental warmth of the state, as well as its deep roots.

DEVILED EGGS

ELIZABETH M. WILLIAMS | MAKES 12

6 large hard-boiled eggs, peeled
¼ cup mayonnaise
2 teaspoons extra virgin olive oil or softened sweet butter
1 tablespoon Dijon mustard
¼ teaspoon salt
¼ teaspoon pepper
1 teaspoon sweet paprika
6 black olives, cut in half

Use a sharp knife to cut each egg in half lengthwise. Gently remove the yolks and put them into a 1-quart bowl. To the yolks, add the mayonnaise, olive oil, mustard, salt, and pepper. With a fork or the back of a spoon, mash the ingredients together until they form a smooth paste. Taste a tiny amount and adjust for salt and pepper.

Place the egg yolk paste in a self-closing sandwich bag. Squeeze the paste into one corner, cut the tip off that corner, and evenly squeeze portions of the paste into each egg-white depression where a yolk had been. Place the paprika into a small strainer and lightly dust the filled eggs. Stand an olive half in each yolk. Serve immediately or refrigerate, covered, up to 8 hours.

DELTA TAMALES

JENNIE MERRILL BOUDREAUX | MAKES ABOUT 4 DOZEN

There is a spicy debate surrounding the Mississippi origins of this economical and nutritious food. Some argue that tamales arrived in the early twentieth century when migrant workers were brought from Mexico to labor in Mississippi's cotton fields. Others say they can be traced back to the U.S.–Mexican war. Or maybe they were derived from an African dish called "cush," or perhaps this combination of cornmeal and meat was a legacy of Indigenous Native American cuisine.

Today, a Mississippi tamale is usually made with cornmeal and cooked either by boiling in spiced liquid or by steaming. Although chefs are returning to using corn husks, parchment paper was used through the later part of the twentieth century, because corn husks were not always available. For generations, tamales have been an easily transportable, delicious pocket food, primarily prepared and eaten by Mississippi's African American population, particularly in the Delta region. Referenced in the songs "Delta Blues" and "They're Red Hot" by the blues musician and songwriter Robert Johnson, hot tamales have an undeniably important place in Mississippi culinary history.

In the past, tamales were eaten plain, especially when consumed in the fields. Today, many people dress them with crema, salsa (*verde* or *roja*), and cheese.

Chicken Filling (recipe follows)
Sauce (recipe follows)
Corn Flour Dough (recipe follows)
4 dozen (9″ x 9″ x 3.5″) paper tamale wrappers
For serving: optional crema, green or red salsa, or your favorite shredded cheese

CHICKEN FILLING

5 cups water
2 yellow onions, each cut in quarters
5 whole, unpeeled garlic cloves
1 teaspoon salt
2 pounds boneless, skinless chicken breasts (about 6) or thighs (about 8)
3 bay leaves
2 teaspoon dried oregano

Combine the water, onion, garlic, and salt in a 2-quart pot and bring to a boil. Add the chicken, bay leaves, and oregano, and decrease heat to a simmer. Cook the chicken, partially covered, until it is thoroughly cooked and tender, about 45 minutes. Add more water as needed. Check for doneness by slipping a knife into the chicken. It should be tender, and there should be no pink juices or meat.

Remove the pot from the heat. Allow the chicken to cool in the broth. When it is cool enough to handle, remove the chicken to a cutting board and reserve the broth. Using two forks, shred the chicken and set it aside. Strain the broth to use as stock in the sauce and corn flour dough.

SAUCE

2 tablespoons olive oil
2 large onions, minced
5 cloves garlic, minced
½ cup chicken broth, reserved from boiling chicken
⅓ cup chili powder
⅓ cup paprika
4 tablespoons ground cumin (preferably from toasted cumin seeds)
4 tablespoons garlic powder
2 tablespoons dried oregano
4 teaspoons smoked paprika (optional)
2 teaspoons cayenne pepper, or to taste
Kosher salt and freshly ground black pepper, to taste

Heat the oil in a sauté pan over medium heat. When the oil is hot, add the onion and sauté until limp and translucent, about 8 minutes. Add the garlic and stir 30 seconds. Add the broth, chili powder, paprika, cumin, garlic powder, oregano, smoked paprika, and cayenne. Season with salt and pepper. Cook until the sauce thickens, about 5 minutes. Add the shredded chicken to the sauce, stir to coat, and cook 3 more minutes. Adjust the seasoning and set aside.

CORN FLOUR DOUGH

1 pound (4 sticks) unsalted butter, at room temperature
5 cups masa harina or corn flour
1 tablespoon, plus 1 teaspoon baking powder
1 tablespoon kosher salt
Chicken stock, as needed

Add the butter to the bowl of a stand mixer and beat on medium for 2 minutes.

In a large bowl, whisk together the corn flour, baking powder, and salt. Add ½ cup of the flour mixture to the creamed butter and mix on low until combined. Add another half-cup of the flour mixture and mix well. Mix in 1 cup flour mixture and then 3 tablespoons of stock. Add the rest of the corn flour mixture a half-cup at a time, adding more stock if the mixture seems dry. The final dough should feel slightly sticky and pliable. It should not feel dry.

Assembly

Place a tamale wrapper on a flat work surface. With your fingers, thinly spread about 2 tablespoons dough into a rectangle on the tamale wrapper, leaving the narrow end of the wrapper with about a half-inch uncovered. The rectangle should be as wide as the narrow part of the wrapper.

Spoon 2 tablespoons of chicken filling in a vertical line down the center of the rectangle. Roll the paper so that you wrap the dough around the filling like a cigarette. Press the dough lightly to seal the seam and then roll the paper tightly around the cigarette shape. Fold the narrow end of the wrapper to make a tight package. Tie a string around the middle of the tamale to keep it from unwrapping during steaming. Repeat until all the dough and filling are used.

Steaming

In a tamale steamer or a pot with a deep steamer tray or basket, add enough water until it is about 1 inch below the steamer tray. Bring to a boil; then reduce heat to a simmer. Place the tamales upright in the basket, with their open ends facing up. (The tamales should be close enough to stay upright, but don't pack them so tightly that they have no room to expand.) Place a piece of parchment paper over the top of the tamales and cover the pot.

Cook 90 minutes. Make sure that the water does not evaporate. If the water gets low, add hot water and bring back to a simmer. Tamales are done when the paper peels off easily, releasing the dough. If they are not cooked after 90 minutes, cook 20 more minutes, and try the paper test again.

Remove the pot from the heat. Let the tamales rest in the pot 5–10 minutes. To remove the first few tamales, work tongs down to the bottom of the steam basket and remove the whole basket. After a few tamales have been removed, the rest will come out easily. Tamales break easily, so be careful when handling. Serve warm with your favorite accompaniments.

FRIED CATFISH WITH COMEBACK SAUCE

TRES WILSON | MAKES 4 SERVINGS

The distinctive Mississippi condiment Comeback Sauce traces its origins to Jackson, the state capital, in the 1930s. First served as a salad dressing at either the Rotisserie or the Mayflower restaurant, the sauce is now used on everything from hamburgers to fried seafood. Ingredients vary from cook to cook, but the base is mayonnaise, ketchup, and chili sauce flavored with Worcestershire sauce, onion, and garlic.

1 pound fresh catfish filets
1 cup yellow mustard
⅔ cup masa
¼ cup all-purpose flour
2 teaspoons salt
1 teaspoon ground black pepper
1 teaspoon cayenne
1 quart vegetable oil
Lemon wedges, for garnish
Paprika
For serving: lemon wedges, paprika, and Comeback Sauce (recipe follows)

Trim the catfish filets so that no piece is longer than 4 inches. Place in a bowl and cover with the mustard, making sure it coats every surface of the fish. Cover the bowl with plastic wrap and refrigerate 1 hour and up to 3 hours.

Place the masa, flour, salt, black pepper, and cayenne in a quart-size paper or self-closing plastic bag. Close and shake the bag to mix thoroughly. Place 2 catfish filets in the bag. Close the bag and shake to coat the filets. Set coated fish aside on a plate. Repeat with all the filets.

Heat the oil in a deep fryer or a cast-iron skillet until it sizzles when a pinch of the coating is dropped in or when it reaches 340°F. Carefully place a few filets into the hot oil. Do not crowd them. Cook until the sizzling stops and the fish is golden brown, about 4 minutes. Turn and cook on the other side, about another 4 minutes. Drain on a wire rack. Repeat with remaining fish.

Place the hot fried fish on a platter and garnish with the lemon wedges. Sprinkle with paprika and serve Comeback Sauce on the side.

COMEBACK SAUCE

MAKES 2½ CUPS

- 1 cup mayonnaise (preferably Duke's)
- 1 cup ketchup
- ½ cup chili garlic sauce
- 3 tablespoons Dijon mustard
- 2 tablespoons sugar
- 1 tablespoon hot sauce
- 2 teaspoons Worcestershire sauce
- Salt and pepper, to taste

Add all the ingredients to a large bowl and whisk until completely incorporated. Place into jars and refrigerate. Use for dipping, on sandwiches, and as salad dressing.

Photo courtesy of Colleen Atherton-Hollier.

POT ROAST

STEPHANIE BOTTOM | MAKES 8 TO 10 SERVINGS

This old-time version of Mississippi pot roast is baked in the oven, unlike the modern fad that is made with seasoning packets and braised in a slow cooker.

3-pound beef rump or shoulder roast
Salt and pepper, to taste
2 teaspoons dried thyme
¼ cup olive oil
2½ cups rich beef stock
1 (12-ounce) bottle beer
2 bay leaves
2 pounds new potatoes, cut in half
6 carrots, peeled and cut into fourths
1 large onion, coarsely chopped
For serving: hot crusty bread

Preheat the oven to 350°F. Dry the roast with a paper towel. Season liberally on all sides with salt, pepper, and thyme. In a large Dutch oven, heat the olive oil over medium-high heat. Brown the roast well on all sides. Add the stock, beer, and bay leaves. Cover the pot and bake 2 hours.

Remove from the oven and nestle the potatoes, carrots, and onion around the roast. Cover and cook another 2 hours. Then remove the pot from the oven and let rest 10 minutes. Serve the roast and vegetables in bowls with crusty bread.

POTATO SALAD

MIKIE HAYES | MAKES 10 TO 12 SERVINGS (START A DAY AHEAD)

6–8 large eggs
5 pounds russet, Yukon gold, or red potatoes
Oil to rub on the boiled potatoes
2 cups Miracle Whip or 1 cup Miracle Whip and 1 cup creamy mayonnaise, such as Duke's or Hellmann's
¼ cup granulated sugar
1½ tablespoons yellow mustard or 2 tablespoons Durkee Famous Sauce
1 tablespoon apple cider vinegar
Salt and pepper, to taste
3 peeled celery stalks, diced small
1 medium sweet onion, diced small
½ cup bread and butter pickles, chopped small
6–8 shakes paprika
10 pitted black olives, sliced thin

The day before, hard-boil and peel the eggs. Refrigerate them. The day you make the potato salad, medium-chop the cooked eggs and set aside.

If potatoes are large, cut them into halves. Cover potatoes in well-salted cold water and bring to a boil in a large stockpot. Reduce heat and cook until fork tender, about 20–25 minutes. Drain in a colander. Pat dry and peel the potatoes. Rub the outside of each thoroughly with oil.

Cut the potatoes into ½–¾-inch bite-sized pieces. (They don't have to be a uniform size.) Put the potatoes in a large bowl. In another bowl, blend together the Miracle Whip, sugar, mustard, vinegar, and salt and pepper to taste. Coat the potatoes with the mayonnaise mixture.

Fold in the celery, onions, and pickles. Gently but thoroughly stir in the hard-boiled eggs. Sprinkle the top with paprika and garnish with black olives. Potato salad really needs to be chilled, so refrigerate at least 6 hours. It's even better when chilled overnight.

CARAMEL CAKE

MATT KONIGSMARK | MAKES 1 (8-INCH) 3-LAYER CAKE

This is the cake Matt Konigsmark's great-grandmother, Sally Hull Weltner, baked for birthdays. For Matt's birthday, his mother made this cake with his grandmother Mimi's caramel icing.

BASIC LAYER CAKE

3 cups all-purpose flour
2 teaspoons baking powder
2 cups granulated sugar
1 cup (2 sticks) butter, softened
4 eggs, yolks and whites separated
1 cup milk, at room temperature
1 teaspoon vanilla extract

Preheat the oven to 300°F. Grease and flour 3 (8-inch) round or square cake pans. In a medium-sized bowl, sift together the flour and baking powder. In a large bowl, use medium mixer speed to cream together the sugar, butter, and egg yolks until light, about 3 minutes. Add the flour mixture by thirds to the creamed butter mixture, alternating with the milk. Add the vanilla.

Beat the egg whites until stiff. Fold the beaten egg whites into the batter. Divide the batter among the three prepared pans and bake until the centers spring back when lightly touched, 25 to 30 minutes. Let sit in the pans for 5 minutes. Remove to racks and cool the cakes completely. Fill and ice with caramel icing.

CARAMEL ICING

3 cups granulated sugar, divided
1½ cups whole milk
½ cup (1 stick) real butter (not margarine)

In a large saucepan stir together 2½ cups sugar and the milk. Bring to a bare simmer. Meanwhile, caramelize the remaining ½ cup sugar by placing it in a small heavy skillet set over low heat. Stir gently and constantly. At about 2 minutes the sugar should be melted. Keep stirring and watch it carefully. At 3 to 4 minutes, it will begin to darken. Remove the skillet from the heat and continue to stir. The residual heat in the pan will keep darkening the sugar. When the sugar is dark brown, stir it into the simmering sugar and milk mixture.

Cook the mixture on medium heat until it just reaches the soft ball stage, 235°F, about 20 minutes. Remove from the heat at once and stir in butter and let cool. Add vanilla and beat with a hand mixer until the icing thickens and is spreadable.

HONEYSUCKLE COLLINS

LAURA BELLUCCI | MAKES 1 COCKTAIL

10 small lemon balm leaves, plus 1 for garnish
¾ ounce Cocktail & Sons Ginger Honey Syrup
¾ ounce lemon juice
Ice cubes
1½ ounces Cathead Honeysuckle Vodka
4 ounces club soda

In a Collins glass, add lemon balm, syrup, and lemon juice. Muddle gently. Add ice and vodka. Top with club soda and stir. Rub the remaining lemon balm sprig between your fingers and drop in the drink for taste and garnish.

HOT TODDY

THE MUSEUM OF THE AMERICAN COCKTAIL | MAKES 1 COCKTAIL

The term "toddy" refers to a type of drink that can be made with any spirit and mixed with hot water, lemon juice or lemon peel, and sugar.

4 ounces hot water
1½ ounces brandy
¼ ounce fresh lemon juice
1 sugar cube, rubbed against the rind of a lemon to infuse it with oils
1 stick cinnamon
For serving: half-slice of lemon

Warm a coffee mug and pour in water, brandy, lemon juice, and a sugar cube. Stir with the cinnamon stick to dissolve the sugar. Garnish with a half-slice of lemon and serve with the cinnamon stick.

An assortment of North Carolina products.

NORTH CAROLINA

BLACK-EYED PEAS, RICE, SWEET TEA, meat and three, and its own special barbecue are essential to the foodways of North Carolina. Red and white slaw, cornbread, catfish, and biscuits are eaten regularly, as are the coast's flounder, red snapper, and bluefish. The state is the nation's leader in sweet potato production. Its geographic and environmental diversity are reflected by the apple orchards of Henderson and the wineries that make merlot and muscadine wine from the Blue Ridge Mountains to the Yadkin Valley.

Native Americans introduced the cornmeal mush that early European settlers often sliced cold and then fried. Fried cornbread was traditionally served with inexpensive black-eyed peas, brought in by enslaved Africans, who also introduced the technology of rice growing to the region. Enslaved Africans also brought okra, which handles the heat of North Carolina summers so well that it almost became native.

In North Carolina, barbecue is serious business, with its varied cultural ties to Indigenous people, Europeans, and African Americans. It is also a politically charged subject, having spawned competing legislative bills to determine an official state barbecue. There are two basic styles of North Carolina barbecue. The Lexington-style sauce, and dip, is based on vinegar and tomato and is mainly used with pork shoulder. The Eastern style is made from vinegar and pepper and is used for whole-hog basting and for dipping.

The soft drink Pepsi, originally called Brad's Drink, was created in 1893 by pharmacist Caleb Bradham in New Bern. The all-American Krispy Kreme Doughnut chain began in Winston-Salem in 1937.

INFAMOUS OLIVE BALLS

STEPHANIE BOTTOM | MAKES 36 HORS D'OEUVRES

This little nibble often appears at southern cocktail hours.

4 dozen large pimento-stuffed green olives
5 ounces grated cheddar cheese
½ cup (1 stick) butter, softened
1½ cups all-purpose flour
Pinch of salt

Drain the olives well. In a large bowl, mix the cheese and butter together. Thoroughly mix in the flour and salt. Divide the dough into 48 pieces. Use your hand to flatten each piece. Fully cover each olive with a piece of dough. Place the covered olives on a parchment-lined cookie sheet and refrigerate 2 hours.

When ready to bake, preheat the oven to 400°F. Bake until the dough begins to brown, about 15 minutes. Serve immediately.

PULLED PORK

MADDIE HAYES | MAKES 12 SERVINGS

3–4 pounds pork butt or pork shoulder
12-ounce pilsner or light lager, something you would drink
1 large white onion, quartered
¼ cup apple cider vinegar
2 tablespoons local honey
1 tablespoon kosher salt
Freshly ground black pepper, to taste
Carolina Gold Sauce (recipe on page 188)
For serving: your favorite vinegar-based barbecue sauce, buns, and coleslaw

Preheat the oven to 300°F. Place the pork in a cast-iron Dutch oven or an oven-safe pot with a lid. Add the beer, onion, and vinegar. Drizzle in the honey. Season with salt and pepper. Cover with the lid and bake until the pork is tender and falling apart and can be shred easily with a fork, at least 4 hours. Check every 30 minutes to an hour to make sure nothing is sticking to the pot's sides or burning.

Turn the oven temperature up to 425°F and take the lid off the pot. Cook the pork until the liquid is reduced and the top of the meat has caramelized, about 1 to 2 hours. The pork should remain juicy. Toss in the barbecue sauce and serve warm on buns and topped with coleslaw.

TRI-COLOR SLAW

ELIZABETH M. WILLIAMS | MAKES 6–8 SERVINGS

1 small head green cabbage
½ head red cabbage
3 yellow bell peppers
1 cup mayonnaise
⅓ cup white wine vinegar
¼ cup olive oil
1 clove garlic, minced
1 teaspoon salt
1 teaspoon black pepper

Cut the green cabbage in half and remove the core. Slice both halves finely with a large knife or on a mandolin. Place in a large bowl. Remove the core from the red cabbage and slice into thin slices. Add to the bowl. Remove the seeds and core from the bell peppers. Slice very thinly lengthwise and add to the bowl.

Make the dressing in a quart jar by adding the mayonnaise, vinegar, olive oil, garlic, salt, and pepper. Screw on the jar's lid and shake vigorously. Coat the cabbage mixture with the dressing. Refrigerate at least an hour before serving.

SWEET POTATO CASSEROLE

MIKIE HAYES · MAKES 4 TO 6 SERVINGS

To cook the sweet potatoes, you can peel, cube, and boil them, but the method that yields the sweetest, best-textured potato is baking or roasting.

4 large sweet potatoes
Cooking spray
1 cup (2 sticks butter), melted and divided
1 cup dark brown sugar, packed and divided
½ cup milk
2 large eggs, beaten
1 teaspoon pure vanilla extract
A healthy pinch of salt
½ cup all-purpose flour
1 cup chopped pecans
2½ cups mini-marshmallows

Preheat the oven to 375°F. Wash, dry, and prick potatoes all over. Spray them with cooking spray. Place sweet potatoes on a baking sheet and bake until tender, about 45–50 minutes.

When cool, spoon the sweet potato flesh into a large bowl. Drop oven temperature to 350°F and coat a 9 × 13-inch baking dish with cooking spray. To the potatoes add ½ cup butter, ½ cup brown sugar, milk, eggs, vanilla, and salt, and mix until smooth. Pour into the prepared dish.

In a bowl, combine flour, remaining ½ cup butter, and remaining ½ cup brown sugar. Stir in pecans and spread topping evenly over sweet potatoes. Top with marshmallows. Bake until golden, approximately 30 minutes. Serve warm.

CANE SYRUP CORNBREAD

COLLEEN ALLERTON-HOLLIER | MAKES 8 TO 10 SERVINGS

This recipe calls for a blend of different flours, and it is worth the trouble! Potato flour is a common ingredient in the Carolinas, and it yields a supremely tender crumb. The whole-wheat flour attributes a wholesome color and flavor. You could use only all-purpose flour, but it wouldn't be as special.

¾ cup (1½ sticks) butter, plus more for topping
1 cup, plus 2 tablespoons buttermilk
1 cup, plus 1 tablespoon yogurt
⅓ cup cane syrup, plus more for topping
1 cup cornmeal
½ cup whole-wheat flour
2 tablespoons, plus 1 teaspoon potato flour
3 tablespoons all-purpose flour
1 tablespoon, plus 1 teaspoon baking powder
2 teaspoons kosher salt
½ teaspoon baking soda
3 large eggs, room temperature

Preheat the oven to 350°F. Place the butter in a 10-inch cast-iron skillet or 2-quart saucier set over medium heat. Stirring occasionally, let the butter brown until it's a deep golden color. Set aside to cool slightly.

In a medium bowl, mix together buttermilk, yogurt, and cane syrup until smooth. In a smaller bowl, sift together cornmeal, whole-wheat flour, potato flour, all-purpose flour, baking powder, salt, and baking soda. Stream brown butter into the wet ingredients, whisking until smooth. Whisk in eggs. Whisk in dry ingredients, and then use a rubber spatula to completely combine the mixture. Batter will be thick and lumpy, and that's okay.

Use the same cast-iron skillet that the butter was browned in or grease a 10-inch cake pan. Bake until a toothpick inserted in the center comes out mostly clean, about 30–45 minutes. Allow cornbread to cool 5 minutes, and then smear with as much butter and cane syrup as you see fit. Serve warm. Will keep wrapped tightly in plastic for about 5 days at room temperature or 7 days in the refrigerator. To reheat, griddle slices of cornbread in a pan with butter.

KRISPY KREME BREAD PUDDING

MADDIE HAYES | MAKES 20 SERVINGS

In 1937, Vernon Rudolph bought a secret yeast-raised doughnut recipe from a French New Orleans chef. He then started the first Krispy Kreme doughnut shop in Winston-Salem, selling to local grocery stores from his rented building. The smell of the doughnuts attracted so many customers that he decided to build a window that opened directly to passersby on the street. The first retail-only location opened in Greensboro in 1989. The company has since expanded to include international locations.

6 large eggs, beaten
¾ cup brown sugar
2 teaspoons vanilla extract
1 teaspoon ground cinnamon
½ teaspoon salt
1 pinch ground nutmeg
3 cups whole milk
¼ cup (½ stick) butter, melted
10 Krispy Kreme doughnuts, cut into 2-inch cubes

Preheat the oven to 375°F. Lightly butter a 3-quart baking dish. In a mixing bowl, beat together the eggs, sugar, vanilla, cinnamon, salt, and nutmeg. Pour in milk and melted butter; mix well. Add doughnut cubes and combine thoroughly. Pour into the prepared baking dish, making sure the doughnut pieces are fully saturated. Bake until golden brown, 30 to 45 minutes. Your kitchen should smell like a bakery! Serve hot, but this is also delicious at room temperature.

CHEERWINE PUNCH

ELIZABETH M. WILLIAMS | MAKES 3½ QUARTS

Cheerwine is a soft drink specific to North Carolina. Invented in 1917 during a sugar shortage, the carbonated beverage is made with a cherry syrup that imparts a deep-red color. Cheerwine is not as sweet as many modern soft drinks. It mixes well with other flavors.

4 cups Cheerwine
4 cups sparkling wine
4 cups unsweetened pineapple juice
1 cup curaçao
10 drops orange bitters
2 cups ice cubes
For garnish: 2 sliced oranges

Mix all the liquid ingredients in a large punch bowl. Just before serving, add the ice. Float the orange slices on top for garnish. Serve in punch cups.

HIBISCUS TEA

SERIGNE MBAYE | MAKES 12 (8-OUNCE) SERVINGS

6 quarts water
2 quarts dried hibiscus flowers, divided
1 quart granulated sugar (depending on how sweet you like it)
3 cups fresh mint, divided, plus additional for garnish
½ cup lime juice
For serving: ice cubes

Bring the water to a boil and add 1 quart dried hibiscus flowers, sugar, and 1½ cups mint. Return to a boil and cook until sugar dissolves. Remove from heat and steep 15 minutes.

Stir in the remaining quart dried hibiscus flowers and the remaining 1½ cups mint. Cover and let sit 30 minutes. Strain into a pitcher and stir in lime juice. Chill.

When ready to serve, pour over ice in tall glasses and garnish with a sprig of mint.

Hasty Bake products, well known in Oklahoma,
and other barbecue products anchor the Oklahoma exhibit.

OKLAHOMA

OKLAHOMA BOASTS HARDY FOLKS who have raised cattle, lived on the wind-swept plains, and made do. This state was the setting for John Steinbeck's *The Grapes of Wrath*. The images of the Dust Bowl and the grim faces of those who left to find work come to mind for many, but Oklahoma is so much more.

The Indigenous population is diverse, with Native Americans whose ancestors have lived on the land since prehistoric times and Native People who were relocated from other parts of the United States. They all bring their foodways to the modern table. They certainly bring the three sisters: corn, beans, and squash. They also make sofky, a stew made of cornmeal and bits of meat, and kunuhchee, a soup made from hickory nuts. The Five Tribes of Eastern Oklahoma have a long-standing tradition of gathering during wild onion season (February to April) for community and private dinners. Of course, wild onions are served, often scrambled in eggs. Other dishes are offered, such as hominy and hickory nut soup, depending on the traditions of the hosts.

Like so much of the rest of the South, Oklahoma's food is a mix of Native American, African, and European cuisines, as well as the food of more recently arrived groups. Whether it is Jell-O salad or fried pork chops, the food identity of Oklahoma is based on a combination of what the state has to offer and exposure to foods brought by settlers and immigrants.

Today's Oklahomans claim that the foods that traditionally represent their state are chicken-fried steak, barbecue, and chili. Many residents also have fond memories of brown candy, a cross between pralines and fudge.

PEPPERED BEEF TENDERLOIN WITH MUSTARD & HORSERADISH SAUCE

STEPHANIE BOTTOM | MAKES 8 TO 10 SERVINGS

1 beef tenderloin
6 or more teaspoons coarsely ground black pepper
2 teaspoons kosher salt
1 cup coarsely chopped fresh parsley, leaves only
3 tablespoons Dijon mustard
2 tablespoons softened butter
For serving: Mustard and Horseradish Sauce (recipe follows)

Preheat the oven to 450°F. Liberally season the beef with black pepper and salt. In a bowl, mix together the parsley, mustard, and butter. (If your tenderloin is large, you may need to double the parsley/butter mixture.) Generously rub the parsley mixture all over the beef.

Roast, uncovered, until a meat thermometer registers 130°F for very rare, about 35 minutes. For medium rare, the thermometer should register 145°F. Remove from the oven and rest 10 minutes. Slice and serve with mustard and horseradish sauce.

MUSTARD & HORSERADISH SAUCE

MAKES 1¼ CUPS

1 cup sour cream
3 tablespoons Dijon mustard
2 tablespoons prepared horseradish

Whisk ingredients together in a small bowl. Cover and refrigerate up to 3 days.

Photo courtesy of Dee Lavigne.

FRIED OKRA WITH JONES SAUCE

ELIZABETH M. WILLIAMS | MAKES 1 POUND FRIED OKRA

1 pound small raw okra
2 cups buttermilk
¼ cup hot sauce
2 teaspoons salt
1 tablespoon black peppercorns
½ teaspoon dried thyme
¼ teaspoon dried tarragon
1 bay leaf
4 cups all-purpose flour
4 cups masa
¾ cup cornmeal
½ cup cornstarch
1½ teaspoons seasoned salt
Peanut oil for frying
For serving: Jones Sauce (recipe follows) or your favorite dipping sauce

Slice okra to the desired size. In a large bowl, combine buttermilk, hot sauce, and salt. Soak the okra in the buttermilk mixture at least 15 minutes and up to 30 minutes.

While the okra is soaking, use a spice or coffee grinder to grind together the peppercorns, thyme, tarragon, and bay leaf. In a large bowl, combine the spice mixture with the flour, masa, cornmeal, cornstarch, and seasoned salt.

Heat 2 inches oil in a deep fryer or large pot to 375°F. After the okra has soaked for at least 15 minutes, remove from buttermilk and dredge in the dry flour mixture. Toss to coat evenly. Shake off excess flour and drop directly into the hot oil. Cook until crispy and golden brown. Serve hot with Jones Sauce.

JONES SAUCE

MAKES 4 CUPS

The origin of this sweet, creamy sauce is elusive. Nevertheless, it is a great dip for fried vegetables, especially fried potatoes and fried sweet potatoes.

1 cup apple cider vinegar
⅓ cup honey
16 ounces Greek yogurt
½ cup mayonnaise
⅓ cup chili garlic sauce
2¼ teaspoons paprika
1½ teaspoons salt
1½ teaspoons ground black pepper
¾ teaspoon garlic powder

Combine vinegar and honey in a small pan, and simmer over low heat until slightly thickened, about 15 minutes. Remove from heat and let cool.

Meanwhile, in a large bowl, combine the yogurt, mayonnaise, chili sauce, paprika, salt, pepper, and garlic powder. Pour in the cooled honey mixture and mix thoroughly.

CREAMED GREENS

STEPHANIE BOTTOM | MAKES 4-6 SERVINGS

This is a modern take on traditional Spinach Madeleine or creamed spinach casserole.

2½ pounds cleaned spinach or other greens
½ cup (1 stick) butter
1 onion, finely chopped
¼ cup all-purpose flour
1 cup evaporated milk
¾ cup shredded Monterey Jack pepper cheese
2 teaspoons celery salt
2 teaspoons garlic powder
2 teaspoons Worcestershire sauce
2 teaspoons lemon juice
1 teaspoon salt
1 teaspoon ground black pepper
Dash of cayenne pepper
1 cup buttered breadcrumbs

Preheat the oven to 350°F. Cook spinach in salted boiling water until wilted and tender, about 4 minutes. (Other types of greens may take longer to cook.) Drain well, reserving 1 cup of cooking liquid. Melt the butter in a large skillet set over medium heat. Add the onion and sauté until soft, about 5 minutes. Add the flour and cook, stirring constantly, for 2 minutes. Add the evaporated milk and reserved cooking liquid. Cook, stirring occasionally, until thick.

Add the cheese, celery salt, garlic powder, Worcestershire sauce, lemon juice, salt, black pepper, and cayenne. Stir until the cheese is melted and the mixture is smooth. Add the greens and stir well. Place into a buttered 9 × 13-inch casserole dish. Top with breadcrumbs and bake 1 hour. Let sit 10 minutes before serving.

CRUSTY BREAD

STEPHANIE BOTTOM | MAKES 1 LOAF

1 envelope active dry yeast
1 cup warm water (110–115°F)
2 tablespoons sugar
2 tablespoons vegetable oil, plus more for oiling bowl and pan
3–3¼ cups bread flour
1½ teaspoons salt
Cornmeal
1 egg white
1 teaspoon cold water

Empty the yeast packet into a large mixing bowl, and add the warm water, sugar, and vegetable oil. Stir together and let sit 20 minutes.

Add 3 cups flour and mix thoroughly. Add more flour if necessary to form a stiff dough. Sprinkle flour on a hard work surface and knead until the dough is pliable and smooth, about 10 minutes. Roll dough into a ball and place in a greased bowl, making sure that the top of the dough is oiled. Cover with a towel and place in a warm area until doubled in bulk, about 1 hour. Gently punch down the dough and return it to the bowl. Cover and let it rise again 30 minutes.

About 15 minutes before the dough has risen the second time, preheat the oven to 375°F. Remove the dough from the bowl and lay it on a floured work surface. Either roll or stretch by hand until the dough forms a 16 × 16-inch square. Roll the dough jellyroll style to form a long loaf.

Grease a sheet pan and sprinkle it with cornmeal. Place the dough seam side down on the pan. Mix the egg white with the cold water and brush it on the top of the bread. Take a sharp knife and make several slashes across the top of the dough. Bake until golden brown, 25–30 minutes. Cool on a wire rack and serve.

SCALLOPED YUKON GOLD & SWEET POTATO GRATIN

STEPHANIE BOTTOM | MAKES 8 TO 10 SERVINGS

1 ½ pounds medium Yukon Gold potatoes
1 ½ pounds red-skinned sweet potatoes
2 cups heavy whipping cream
¼ cup (½ stick) butter
2 cloves garlic, minced
1 tablespoon chopped Italian parsley
1 tablespoon chopped fresh rosemary
1 tablespoon chopped sage
1 tablespoon chopped thyme
1½ teaspoons salt
¾ teaspoon freshly ground black pepper
1¼ cups coarsely grated Gruyère or Emmentaler cheese, packed

Fill a large bowl with cold water. Peel the potatoes and cut into ⅛-inch thick rounds. Place the potatoes in the bowl of water and let sit at least 1 hour and up to 4 hours. (This removes excess starch.) Drain potatoes and pat dry.

Preheat the oven to 400°F. Combine cream, butter, and garlic in a pan and bring to a low simmer. Cook 2 minutes and then remove from heat. Combine the chopped herbs in a bowl.

Butter a 9 × 13-inch baking dish and transfer half the potatoes to the dish. Sprinkle with salt and pepper and then half the herb mixture. Add half the cheese, covering the layer of potatoes evenly. Repeat and make a second layer with remaining potatoes, herbs, and cheese.

Pour cream mixture over the top. Cover with aluminum foil and bake 30 minutes. Remove foil and continue baking until the gratin is golden and liquid is absorbed, another 20–25 minutes. Cool 10 minutes and then serve.

COCONUT CREAM PIE

MADDIE HAYES | MAKES 1 (9-INCH) PIE

This coconut cream pie is heavily inspired by Cattlemen's Steakhouse in Oklahoma City.

4 large eggs, yolks and whites separated
¼ cup cornstarch
1 (14-ounce) can full-fat coconut milk
1 cup whole milk or half-and-half
⅔ cup, plus ¼ cup granulated sugar
¼ teaspoon salt
1½ teaspoons vanilla extract, divided
1 cup sweetened shredded coconut
2 tablespoons salted or unsalted butter
1 (9-inch) pie crust (store bought or homemade), baked, perforated, and cooled
¼ teaspoon cream of tartar

In a small mixing bowl, whisk together the egg yolks and cornstarch. Set aside. In a saucepan, combine coconut milk, whole milk, ⅔ cup sugar, and salt. Place on a medium flame and cook, stirring often, until the mixture reaches a low boil (bubbles appear around the edges). Be careful not to scorch the milk. Remove from heat and stir in 1 teaspoon vanilla.

Temper the eggs by slowly pouring ½ cup of the hot milk mixture into the egg mixture, whisking constantly so the eggs don't scramble. Whisk gently as you slowly add the egg mixture to the milk mixture in the saucepan. Place over low heat and stir constantly until the mixture thickens, about 5 minutes. Remove pudding from the heat, and gently stir in the coconut and butter.

Pour the pudding into the baked pie crust. Gently shake the pie on the table to make sure the filling has settled. Cover the pie with plastic wrap. The plastic should make direct contact with the surface of the pie to prevent a skin from forming. Chill the pie a few hours and up to overnight before topping with meringue.

Once the pie is cold, preheat the oven to 350°F. Make the meringue in a standing mixer set on high speed by beating together the egg whites, ¼ cup sugar, and cream of tartar until the mixture forms soft peaks. Beat in the remaining ½ teaspoon vanilla a few seconds. Do not overbeat.

Spread the meringue on top of the pie and bake until golden brown, 15 to 20 minutes. Rotate as necessary. Cool completely. Store in the refrigerator up to 5 days.

Photo courtesy of Dee Lavigne.

PECAN PIE COOKIES

DEE LAVIGNE | MAKES 24 COOKIES

Here are five tips for making beautiful cookies: (1) Refrigerate the dough before baking to prevent the cookies from spreading out too thin. The longer the better: a minimum of two hours produces the best results. (2) To get uniformly sized cookies in the oven quickly, use a cookie scoop. (3) Leave a 2-inch gap on the cookie sheet between cookies so they have room to spread. (4) Preheat the oven before baking to allow cookies to bake evenly. (5) Check your cookies halfway through baking to see if one side is cooking quicker than the other. Rotate if necessary.

2 cups brown sugar, lightly packed
1 cup (2 sticks) salted butter, softened
1 tablespoon vanilla extract
2 large eggs
2 cups all-purpose flour
½ teaspoon salt
½ teaspoon baking soda
2 cups pecan pieces

In a large bowl, use an electric mixer on medium speed to beat brown sugar, butter, and vanilla until fluffy, about 5 minutes. Beat in eggs. Add flour, salt, and baking soda, and mix on low until just combined. Stir in the pecans. Chill the dough for 1 hour.

Preheat the oven to 350°F. Line a cookie sheet with parchment paper. Scoop cookies into 1¼-inch balls or 1-ounce scoops and place 2 inches apart on the cookie sheet. Bake until brown around the edges, 12 to 15 minutes. Cool a minute on the cookie sheet, then remove to a cooling rack.

OKLAHOMA BROWN CANDY

ELIZABETH M. WILLIAMS | MAKES 6 POUNDS CANDY

6 cups granulated sugar, divided
2 cups whole milk or heavy cream
¼ teaspoon baking soda
¼ pound (1 stick) butter
1 teaspoon vanilla
4 cups broken nuts

Place 2 cups sugar into a heavy skillet over low heat, and cook and watch attentively as the sugar melts and begins to caramelize to a light brown. Stir as needed to keep from sticking and scorching. This may take 25 minutes.

Place the remaining 4 cups sugar and the milk into a pot. With 5 minutes left to cook the 2 cups of sugar, bring the pot of milk and sugar to a simmer over low heat, stirring as needed. When the sugar in the skillet becomes caramelized, immediately remove it from the heat. Pour it very slowly in a steady stream into the simmering milk mixture, all the while stirring. Continue cooking without stirring until reaching the soft ball stage when a candy thermometer reads 245°F and no higher than 250°F. Remove from the heat.

Add the baking soda and stir as the mixture foams. Add the butter and continue to stir until the butter is melted. Set aside to cool until mixture reaches 160°F, 20–25 minutes.

Butter a 9×13-inch baking pan. Stir the cooled candy vigorously until the mixture loses its gloss; then stir in the nuts. Quickly spread the candy into the prepared pan. Allow to harden. Cut into 1-inch squares.

WATERMELON LEMONADE

ELIZABETH M. WILLIAMS | MAKES 10 (8-OUNCE) SERVINGS

Lemonade is very much associated with the South. When watermelon is in season, it adds variety to familiar plain lemonade. This cooling drink also makes it possible to use up all the watermelon that is ripening at the same time, conserving lemons for other uses. Remember that the food of the South is often the food of poverty, and nothing would have been thrown away. With that in mind, reserve the watermelon rind to make Watermelon Rind Pickles (page 66).

8 cups cubed, seeded watermelon
7 cups water
1 cup freshly squeezed lemon juice
1 cup granulated sugar
Fresh mint sprigs
Ice cubes

Place the watermelon in a food processor and process until it liquifies. Strain out the pulp. Measure 2 cups juice. Save the remainder for another use.

Stir together the 2 cups watermelon juice, water, lemon juice, and sugar. Bruise a few mint leaves in serving glasses. Add ice and pour in the lemonade. Garnish with more mint.

The influence of Africans, who were enslaved in South Carolina, can be seen in the rice tools as well as the mortar and pestle in the South Carolina exhibit.

SOUTH CAROLINA

THE GULLAH ARE A DISTINCT ETHNIC GROUP that evolved in the coastal lands from North Carolina to northern Florida. The Gullah people are descended from enslaved West Africans who remained isolated after emancipation and therefore developed a unique culture and cuisine. Until well after the 1930s, the homes of many Gullah could only be accessed by boat, greatly reducing outside influences. Many Gullah dishes were intentionally created as one-pot meals. This cuisine includes such foods as okra, beans, greens, corn, rice, game, and seafood.

The rice culture of South Carolina connects just about everyone there to the land. Commercial rice production began in the seventeenth century, and in South Carolina the preferred variety was called Carolina Gold. Through the years, production of Carolina Gold has continued but its popularity has fluctuated. Given the recognition of the importance of plant diversity and our interest in heritage seeds, this old variety is making a comeback.

The traditional food of the city of Charleston is based on contributions from people of African descent, the British, and French Huguenots. Since the state borders the Atlantic Ocean, shrimp, crabs, and oysters are extremely popular, and they show up in dishes such as she-crab soup, deviled crabs, and oyster stew. Oysters are the star of the show at oyster roasts, where they cook in steaming pits, are shoveled onto long tables, and eaten with crackers and sauces.

Some of the modern food crops grown in South Carolina are corn, peanuts, wheat, melons, and peaches. Favorites on dining tables are barbecue, shrimp and grits, cornbread, pimento cheese (made with Duke's Mayonnaise, of course), fried okra, and Frogmore stew. A seasoned medley of boiled shrimp, corn, sausage, and potatoes, Frogmore stew is one of those dishes that crosses the state line and can be found in Georgia, because food is not deterred by neat political boundaries.

LOW-COUNTRY SHRIMP & GRITS

MADDIE HAYES MAKES 4 SERVINGS

4 cups chicken or vegetable stock
1 cup stone-ground grits
1 cup shredded cheddar cheese
6 tablespoons salted butter, divided
2 tablespoons heavy cream
Few dashes hot sauce
Kosher salt and freshly ground black pepper, to taste
½ pound andouille sausage, sliced, then quartered
2 tablespoons olive oil
1 small onion, diced
1 medium red bell pepper, diced
2 cloves garlic, minced
1 tablespoon tomato paste
1 teaspoon Creole seasoning
1 cup diced ripe tomato, with the juice
½ cup dry white wine, something you would drink
Juice of 1 lemon
1 pound shrimp, peeled and deveined
½-1 cup chicken or vegetable stock
2 teaspoons Worcestershire sauce
For garnish: sliced green onions and chopped fresh parsley

For the grits, bring stock to a boil and stir in the grits. Reduce heat to low, cover, and cook until the grits are tender and the liquid has been absorbed, 15–20 minutes. Remove from heat. Add cheese, 4 tablespoons butter, heavy cream, and hot sauce to taste. Stir until melted and evenly distributed. Season to taste with salt and pepper and keep warm.

For the shrimp, add the andouille sausage to a large skillet over medium heat and cook, stirring occasionally until lightly browned, about 5 minutes. Remove the sausage from the skillet. Melt the remaining 2 tablespoons butter. Add the olive oil, then the onion and bell pepper, and sauté until softened, about 3 minutes. Add the garlic and sauté an additional minute. Add the tomato paste and Creole seasoning and cook 1 minute, stirring constantly to ensure that nothing burns. The tomato paste will be a deep rust color.

Deglaze with the tomato and its juice, wine, and lemon juice. Bring to a simmer and cook 2–3 minutes. Add the shrimp and stir constantly until they begin to turn pink, about 2 minutes. Add ½ cup stock, Worcestershire sauce, and hot sauce to taste and cook 2–3 minutes more. Add the andouille sausage back to the skillet and bring to a simmer. Add more stock if needed to make a spoonable sauce that generously coats the shrimp. Season with salt and pepper. On four serving plates, spoon the shrimp and sauce over the warm cheese grits. Sprinkle with green onions and parsley and serve hot.

CAROLINA GOLD RICE PERLOO

ELIZABETH M. WILLIAMS | MAKES 8 TO 10 SERVINGS

This is another Gullah dish with deep roots in the low country. Although it is traditionally made with rice, shrimp, and tomatoes, no two perloos are the same. And don't be surprised if you see the word "perloo" spelled different ways.

6 slices thick-cut bacon
1 large onion, chopped
2 stalks celery, chopped
1 bell pepper, chopped
1 bay leaf
6 cups seafood stock
½ teaspoon ground black pepper
3 cups raw Carolina Gold rice
1½ pounds tomatoes, diced
2 teaspoons salt
5 dashes hot sauce
1½ pounds shrimp, cleaned and peeled
Red pepper flakes

Cook the bacon in a large Dutch oven until it is crisp. Reserving the grease, chop the cooked bacon and set it aside. Cook the onion over medium heat in 3–4 tablespoons of the reserved bacon fat, until it becomes soft, about 5 minutes. Stir in the celery, bell pepper, and bay leaf. Add the seafood stock and black pepper and bring to a slow boil. Add the rice, diced tomatoes, salt, and hot sauce. Bring the mixture back to a boil; then lower the flame and cover the pot. Cook until the rice has absorbed the liquid, 20 minutes.

Remove the lid and add the shrimp. Working quickly, carefully mix it into the rice mixture. Immediately put on the lid and let the heat of the rice cook the shrimp, about five minutes. Remove the lid again, and sprinkle with red pepper flakes and the chopped bacon. Serve warm.

SHE-CRAB SOUP

ELIZABETH M. WILLIAMS | MAKES 4 SERVINGS

½ cup (1 stick) butter
1 shallot, finely diced
1 bay leaf
1 stalk celery, finely diced
2 cloves garlic, finely minced
4 tablespoons all-purpose flour
2 cups Crab Stock (recipe follows), or seafood stock
2 cups whole milk
1 cup half-and-half
5 dashes hot sauce, or to taste
1 pound crabmeat, picked over for shells, divided
1 cup crab fat and roe
1 teaspoon grated orange rind
Salt and pepper, to taste
For serving: chopped chives and dry sherry

In a stock pot over medium heat, melt the butter. Sauté the shallot and bay leaf until the shallot is soft, about 5 minutes. Do not allow it to brown. Add the celery and garlic. Cook 5 minutes. Add the flour and stir 3 minutes. Add the crab stock, milk, and half-and-half. Whisk until thick.

Add the hot sauce. Gently stir in half the crabmeat and all the fat and roe and orange rind. Heat 5 minutes over low heat. Do not let the soup boil.

Taste and adjust for salt and pepper. Remove the bay leaf. Divide the soup among four large soup bowls. Divide the remaining crab meat evenly among the bowls. Garnish with chopped chives. Place the bottle of sherry on the table, encouraging diners to add at least a tablespoon to their bowls.

CRAB STOCK

MAKES ABOUT 1 QUART (PER DOZEN CRABS)

For each dozen uncooked crabs you will need:
8 quarts water
1 bag dry crab boil (purchased from specialty stores or online)
1 onion, cut in half
2 bay leaves
2 stalks celery
Half a lemon

In a stock pot, bring water to a rolling boil. Add the crab boil, onion, bay leaves, and celery and simmer 15 minutes. Add the crabs. They should be completely submerged. After water returns to a boil, cook the crabs about 10 minutes.

Use tongs to remove the crabs from the stock. (When crabs are cool, peel them and use the meat as you wish.) Continue boiling the stock until it has reduced by one-quarter. Strain out the solids through a colander. Crab stock freezes well.

HOPPIN' JOHN

MADDIE HAYES | MAKES 8 SERVINGS (BEGIN THE NIGHT BEFORE)

This dish is traditionally served on New Year's Day to bring prosperity. Dishes of peas and beans served over rice are common all over the South and are rooted in African tradition.

- 2 cups dried black-eyed peas
- 1 smoked ham hock or 8 ounces slab bacon, cut into ¼-inch pieces
- 2 tablespoons extra virgin olive oil
- 1 large onion, chopped
- 1 small green bell pepper, chopped
- 2 celery stalks, chopped
- 2 cloves garlic, chopped
- 2 teaspoons Cajun seasoning
- 2 teaspoons dried thyme
- 2 teaspoons hot sauce
- 1 bay leaf
- 1 jalapeño, sliced lengthwise in half (optional)
- 6 cups chicken broth or water
- Salt and pepper, to taste
- For serving: cooked Carolina Gold rice, Collard Greens (page 198), and green onions

In a large bowl, cover the dried beans with 2 inches water and let soak overnight. The next day, drain the beans and set aside.

If using a ham hock, heat oil in a medium-sized Dutch oven or another large, covered pot over medium-high heat, and cook 15 minutes. If using bacon, cook over medium-low heat, stirring occasionally, until the bacon is crisp, 8–10 minutes. Using a slotted spoon, transfer the ham hock or bacon to a paper-towel–lined plate.

To the same pot, add the onion, bell pepper, and celery and cook, stirring occasionally until they begin to brown, about 5 minutes. Add garlic and cook, stirring often until fragrant, about 1 minute. Add the black-eyed peas, Cajun seasoning, thyme, hot sauce, bay leaf, jalapeño, and ham hock (if using). Pour in broth and bring to a boil. Reduce heat and simmer, uncovered, until beans are tender but not mushy, 1–2½ hours. Stir occasionally.

Drain black-eyed peas and discard the bay leaf. Return the peas to the pot. If using bacon, add it now. If using ham hock, remove it from the pot, let cool slightly, and pull the meat from the bone. Discard the bone and add the meat to the pot. Season beans to taste, and sprinkle with green onions. Serve with low-country rice and collard greens. Sprinkle with additional green onions.

BERNIE'S POPPYSEED BREAD

MADDIE HAYES | MAKES 2 LOAVES

3 cups all-purpose flour
2¼ cups granulated sugar
3 teaspoons baking powder
1½ teaspoons salt
1½ cups whole milk
1 cup neutral oil, like canola or peanut oil
3 large eggs, room temperature
1½ tablespoons poppy seeds
1½ teaspoons butter flavoring
1½ teaspoons almond extract
1 tablespoon vanilla extract

GLAZE

¾ cup confectioners' sugar
¼ cup freshly squeezed orange juice
1 teaspoon vanilla extract
½ teaspoon almond extract

Preheat the oven to 350°F. Grease and flour 2 (9 × 5-inch) loaf pans. In a large bowl, combine the flour, sugar, baking powder, and salt. In a separate small bowl, whisk together the milk, oil, eggs, poppy seeds, butter flavoring, and almond and vanilla extracts. Gently stir the wet ingredients into the dry until combined.

Divide batter between prepared pans. Bake until a toothpick inserted in the center comes out clean, about 55–60 minutes. Cool 10 minutes and then remove from pans to wire racks.

Combine glaze ingredients. With a toothpick, poke small holes in the top of the cakes and drizzle the glaze over the warm loaves. (If you're a more-is-more kind of person, after the first glaze, halve the glaze recipe and make it again, spooning a second round on warm loaves. It will make them extra sweet and moist.)

EAST OF THE COOPER RIVER FRESH PEACH COBBLER

MIKIE HAYES | MAKES 4 TO 6 SERVINGS

South Carolina has a thriving peach industry. An easy way to peel peaches is to cut a shallow *X* on the bottom of each peach and then boil them for thirty seconds. Remove the peaches with a slotted spoon and immediately place into an ice-water bath to stop the cooking process. Peel at the *X*. Overcooking or not cooling peaches can result in a mushy texture.

½ cup (1 stick) salted butter
1 cup all-purpose flour
1⅔ cups granulated sugar, divided
1¾ teaspoons baking powder
Pinch of salt
⅔ cup milk
2 cups peeled and sliced fresh peaches
⅔ cup water
1 tablespoon cornstarch
1 teaspoon pure vanilla extract

Preheat the oven to 400°F. Melt butter in a 9×13-inch baking dish. Spread the butter over the entire bottom and the sides. In a bowl, combine the flour, 1 cup sugar, baking powder, and salt. Stir in the milk. Pour the mixture in the prepared baking dish.

Place the sliced peaches into a large saucepan. Add the water, remaining ⅔ cup sugar, cornstarch, and vanilla. Bring to a boil over medium heat and cook, stirring occasionally until thick, 2–3 minutes. Pour the peach mixture over the batter. Bake 10 minutes. Reduce oven temperature to 375°F, and bake until golden, 20 more minutes.
Serve warm.

CAROLINA GOLD SAUCE

MADDIE HAYES | MAKES ABOUT 1¼ CUPS

German immigrants get the credit for creating this mustard-based sauce that South Carolinians slather on everything from barbecue to hot wings to hushpuppies.

1 cup yellow mustard
¼ cup apple cider vinegar
¼ cup brown sugar, packed
2 tablespoons local honey
½ teaspoon ground black pepper
¼ teaspoon cayenne pepper
¼ teaspoon onion powder
¼ teaspoon garlic powder
Your favorite hot sauce, to taste
Kosher salt, to taste

Add all ingredients to a medium saucepan set over medium heat. Bring to a boil and then reduce to a simmer. Cook, stirring occasionally, until reduced slightly, about 5 minutes. Remove the sauce from the stove and let cool to room temperature. Keeps in the refrigerator up to a week.

SWEET TEA SPRITZ

BRENT ROSEN | MAKES 12 SERVINGS

For friends who don't drink alcohol, this "mocktail" offers more depth and character than the usual non-alcoholic sparkler.

This recipe is based on the Dark and Stormy cocktail. We leave out the rum and add iced tea to make sure the drink isn't cloyingly sweet. You can use cold-brew black tea for this punch. Simply mix the tea bags with cold water, and it brews in minutes. Cold-brew tea is strong enough to be diluted in punch but doesn't have so much caffeine that you turn into a jitterbug.

Mint, lime, lemon, and ginger beer also mix into this drink, turning it into something foreign and familiar all at once. This is a bright, daytime-fresh concoction that will delight the boozeless and boozy alike.

8 cups chilled black tea
5 cups ginger beer
1 cup lemon juice
1 cup lime juice
Ice cubes
4 large mint leaves
For serving, 12 small mint sprigs and 12 lemon twists

In a punch bowl, combine tea, ginger beer, and lemon and lime juices. Add ice cubes and a chiffonade of mint (4 leaves rolled together and finely sliced.) Serve in a Collins glass garnished with a small mint sprig wrapped in a lemon twist.

MAMA TRIED PUNCH

BRENT ROSEN | MAKES 8 SERVINGS

Classic cocktail bartenders love making punch, because punch is older and more traditional than the cocktail. Punch was the original bad-boy drink for sailors and dandies (there were many who made their way to early Charleston), as well as the men and women who associated with them. Modern chains serve punches like this one. One is a gin cocktail called Mother's Ruin. The old British slang for gin was "mother's ruin," because one good night of gin drinking could undue a whole lifetime of Mama's influence.

We call this punch "Mama Tried" in honor of the old gin drinkers and revivalist bartenders who have brought gin punch back into bars. When making this recipe, it's important to remember two things. First, use a dry gin. When punches like this were created, floral gins hadn't been invented yet, and therefore they won't mix well with the other ingredients. Second, because of the champagne and the sparkling water, this punch won't keep forever. Make sure you make small batches; you won't be able to freeze this one.

2¼ cups chilled champagne
1½ cups dry gin
1½ cups freshly squeezed grapefruit juice
¾ cup freshly squeezed lemon juice
¾ cup chilled club soda
¾ cup sweet vermouth
½ cup granulated sugar
For serving: ice cubes and lemon slices

In a punch bowl, mix all the ingredients together, but don't add ice because it will dilute the sitting punch. Serve over ice in footed tumblers or cocktail glasses. Garnish with lemon slices.

From Elvis to barbecue and Piggly Wiggly to GooGoo Clusters,
Tennessee offers up a multitude of influences.

TENNESSEE

TENNESSEE IS A SERIOUS BARBECUE STATE. It celebrates this time-honored way of cooking with an annual barbecue festival known as Memphis in May. Most Tennessee barbecue uses either pork ribs or pork shoulder with a tomato-based sauce.

Farmland covers about 44 percent of Tennessee, yielding many varieties of fresh vegetables, particularly snap beans and tomatoes. Apples grow in all parts of the state. Tennessee also commercially produces corn, wheat, pigs, and livestock.

Virtually every early European family of settlers in Tennessee grew corn as its main source of food. Tennessee is known for corn whiskey. By law, Tennessee's distilled spirit can't be called bourbon, but Jack Daniels and several other distilleries produce brown spirits that can stand up to anything found in Kentucky.

In addition to barbecue and spirits, Tennesseans love sweetened vegetables, greens, any kind of beans, cornbread, hushpuppies, biscuits, and sweet tea. As in much of the South, European and African influences have blended to create "southern" cuisine, which includes the famous meat and three, a meat main dish with three side dishes. Combined with sweet tea, you'll find the traditional meat and three on lunch menus across the state.

Tennessee is home to Moon Pies and Goo Goo Clusters. Lodge Manufacturing Company, the foremost maker of cast-iron cookware, was established in South Pittsburg in 1896.

COMPETITION BABY BACK RIBS

PITMASTER JAMES CRUSE | MAKES 4 SERVINGS

Hickory lump charcoal and cherrywood chunks
2 slabs baby back ribs
Yellow mustard
Dry Rub (recipe follows) or your favorite dry rub
1 cup of your favorite sweet barbecue sauce
½ cup honey

Preheat your smoker to 275–300°F using hickory charcoal and cherry wood chunks.

Trim the ribs and remove the membrane. Apply a light coat of mustard on all sides, followed by a coat of your favorite barbecue rub. Let the ribs sit and sweat a little, and then apply a light dusting of more barbecue rub. Put them in the smoker and cook 1 hour.

Spray the ribs with water and smoke 30 minutes. Remove from the smoker and dust them with more barbecue rub. Wrap each rib slab in two sheets of heavy-duty foil. Return the wrapped ribs to the smoker and cook until the bones feel like they could easily be pulled apart, about 3 to 5 hours altogether.

Meanwhile, make a glaze by combining barbecue sauce and honey in a small saucepan and heat until it comes to a simmer. When the ribs are done, remove the foil and apply the glaze all over. Place the ribs on the smoker until the sauce gets tacky, about 5 minutes. Apply one more coat and cook another 5 minutes. The ribs will now be completely cooked. Remove them from the smoker and let rest 5 minutes before serving.

DRY RUB

MADDIE HAYES | MAKES ABOUT ½ CUP

1½ tablespoons sweet paprika
1½ tablespoons smoked paprika
4 teaspoons kosher salt
2 teaspoons coarsely ground black pepper
2 teaspoons red pepper flakes
2 teaspoons dark brown sugar
1 teaspoon garlic powder
1 teaspoon onion powder

In a bowl, combine all the ingredients. You can double or even triple this mixture and keep it on hand in your pantry.

COUNTRY HAM & RED-EYE GRAVY

ELIZABETH M. WILLIAMS | MAKES 1 TO 2 SERVINGS

1 slice fatty country ham
¾ strong black coffee, simmering
For serving: hot biscuits and fried eggs (optional)

Heat a heavy skillet and add the slice of ham. To render the fat, sauté 6–8 minutes on each side. Remove the ham and set aside. Deglaze the skillet with the hot coffee, scraping to get all the brown bits off the bottom. Cook 2 minutes. Serve immediately over the ham or over hot biscuits and fried eggs.

SUMMER SALAD

CASSIDEE DABNEY | MAKES 6–8 SERVINGS

2 English cucumbers
1 ripe peach, thinly sliced
1 poblano pepper, thinly sliced
1 green tomato, thinly sliced
1 cup Preserved Peppers, plus 2 tablespoons oil (recipe follows)
1 cup basil leaves, plus more for garnish
Lemon juice
Salt and pepper, to taste
4 cups cottage cheese
4 tablespoons Chive Oil (recipe follows)

Peel the cucumbers, slice in half lengthwise, and use a spoon to remove the seeds. (The seeds are great for cocktails or cucumber water.) Use a mandolin to thinly slice the cucumbers. Gently combine the sliced cucumbers, peach slices, poblano pepper slices, tomato slices, preserved peppers, and basil in a large mixing bowl. Drizzle with the oil from the preserved peppers and a sprinkle of lemon juice. Season to taste.

Place a generous spoonful of cottage cheese in the bottom of serving bowls. Season with salt and freshly cracked pepper. Top with the dressed salad and a drizzle of the chive oil. Garnish with additional basil leaves. Serve immediately.

PRESERVED PEPPERS

MAKES 6 CUPS (BEGIN A DAY AHEAD)

6 cups bell or other sweet peppers
3 cups white wine vinegar
¼ cup salt
¼ cup granulated sugar
Pinch of ascorbic acid
Olive oil, to cover

Slice peppers ⅛-inch thick on a mandolin. In a nonreactive bowl, combine the vinegar, salt, sugar, and ascorbic acid. Brine the peppers in the liquid 24 hours. Strain off the liquid. Place peppers in a glass container, cover with olive oil, and cover the container. Store up to 3 months in the refrigerator.

CHIVE OIL

MAKES AS MUCH AS YOU WANT

Puree equal parts chives and vegetable oil in a blender. Pour into a saucepan, place over high heat, and bring to a simmer. Cook 3 minutes. The puree will separate and become bright green. Immediately strain and cool.

COLLARD GREENS

MIKIE HAYES | MAKES 8 SERVINGS

12 cups (2 pounds) collard greens (you can also add mustard greens, turnip greens, and kale)
2 ham hocks or 1 smoked turkey leg
4 slices thick-cut bacon
2 tablespoons olive oil
1 large Vidalia or sweet onion, diced
1 teaspoon finely chopped garlic
1 teaspoon red pepper flakes, or to taste
1 tablespoon smoked paprika
1–2 teaspoons Creole seasoning (I prefer Tony Chachere's or Zatarain's)
5 cups or more chicken broth
1 tablespoon ham-flavored Better than Bouillon-brand seasoning base
Salt and pepper
2–3 teaspoons brown sugar, or to taste
2 teaspoons apple cider vinegar
For serving: hot pepper sauce (I prefer Texas Pete) and a loaf of crusty bread

Fill a clean sink with warm water. Add the whole collard leaves and 2 teaspoons salt, which helps remove grit and sand. Wash the leaves well. Drain the dirty water and repeat the process. It might sound like a lot of work, but greens are sandy and dirty. Place the cleaned greens on paper towels and blot dry. Once dry, move them to a cutting board. De-stem the greens by folding the leaves in half at the spine, then using a sharp knife to cut along the spine, which cuts both sides of the leaf at one time. Roll up several leaves like a cigar and cut them in strips, like a pinwheel sandwich. Chop the greens into bite-sized pieces.

In a large pot, cover the ham hocks fully with water and bring to a boil. Lower the heat and simmer until the meat falls off the bone, about 90 minutes.

In a large pot or Dutch oven, fry the bacon until brown but not crisp. Drain on paper towels. When cool, cut into bite-sized pieces. Add the olive oil to the pot and lower heat to medium. Add the onion and cook until it begins to soften, about 5 minutes. Add the garlic, pepper flakes, and ham hocks and sauté 3 minutes. Add the bacon, smoked paprika, and Creole seasoning and sauté an additional 2 minutes. Add 5 cups chicken broth and ham bouillon. Taste the broth, and then season with salt and pepper if necessary. This would be the time to tweak your seasonings.

Add the chopped greens, stir, and cover. Cook until the greens are cooked down and tender, 2 hours. With about 15 minutes to go, add the brown sugar and apple cider vinegar. Taste and add salt, pepper, and additional brown sugar, if desired. Remove any meat from the ham bones and remove any bones from the pot. Add the meat back in and serve the greens hot with pepper sauce. Do not throw away the pot liquor—it's liquid gold and meant to be sopped up with crusty bread.

MOON PIES

JENNIE MERRILL BOUDREAUX | MAKES 8 SANDWICH COOKIES

The Moon Pie snack was invented in Tennessee by the Chattanooga Bakery, Inc., and was associated with a cheap lunch—an RC Cola and a Moon Pie. During Mardi Gras parades in Mobile, Alabama, riders throw moon pies from floats as favors.

COOKIES

½ cup (1 stick) butter, softened
½ cup granulated sugar
1 large egg
½ cup evaporated milk
½ teaspoon vanilla extract
1 cup all-purpose flour
¼ cup unsweetened cocoa powder
¾ teaspoon baking soda
¼ teaspoon baking powder
¼ teaspoon salt

Preheat the oven to 400°F. Lightly grease a cookie sheet and set aside.

In a large mixing bowl, use the medium mixer speed to cream together butter and granulated sugar, about 3 minutes. Add the egg, evaporated milk, and vanilla, and mix well. In a separate bowl, mix together flour, cocoa powder, baking soda, baking powder, and salt. While stirring with a spoon, add flour mixture slowly to sugar mixture. Mix just until all ingredients are combined.

Drop the dough onto the prepared cookie sheet by rounded tablespoonfuls. Leave at least 3 inches between each: dough will spread as it bakes. Bake until firm when pressed with a finger, 6–8 minutes. Cool at least 1 hour before filling.

MARSHMALLOW FILLING

½ cup (1 stick) butter or margarine, softened
½ cup confectioners' sugar
½ cup marshmallow crème
¼ teaspoon vanilla extract

In a medium bowl, blend together butter, confectioners' sugar, marshmallow crème, and vanilla. Mix until smooth.

Assembly

Spread 1–2 tablespoonfuls of filling on the flat side of a cookie crust. Cover with the flat side of another cookie crust.

APPLE BUTTER

ELIZABETH M. WILLIAMS | MAKES 3 PINTS

Apples are a widely produced crop in Tennessee; an average of six million bushels are farmed annually. Apple butter can be found at corner stores and gas stations during apple season. It is great on oatmeal and toast or even with desserts.

4 cups soft apple cider
8 cups peeled and coarsely chopped apples
1 cup granulated sugar
1 cup dark brown sugar
2 teaspoons cinnamon
¼ teaspoon ground cloves
¼ teaspoon ground allspice
1 tablespoon lemon zest

Place the apple cider in a large pot or Dutch oven. Simmer 20 minutes. Add the apples and simmer until the apples fall apart and the mixture looks like applesauce, about 1 hour.

Stir in the sugar, brown sugar, spices, and zest. Cook an additional 5 minutes or longer if the mixture appears to be too watery. Remove from heat. When the apple butter is cool, transfer it into jars or crocks and refrigerate. Keeps in the refrigerator up to 3 weeks.

APPLE CIDER SPRITZ

BRENT ROSEN | MAKES 12 SERVINGS

This punch is based on the Chimayo, a drink from New Mexico that combines flavors of the border with classic American ingredients like apple cider. This punch keeps extremely well. If you have any left over, you can freeze it.

5 cups Tennessee Whiskey
5 cups unfiltered apple cider
2½ cups freshly squeezed lemon juice
1 cup Crème de Cassis
For serving: ice cubes and lemon slices

In a punch bowl, mix all the main ingredients together. Serve over ice in footed tumblers or cocktail glasses. Garnish with lemon slices.

BOURBON BELLE OLD FASHIONED

JAMES HENSLEY | MAKES 1 COCKTAIL

The mare Bourbon Belle was descended from the sire Bonnie Scotland, the horse on the right side of the Belle Meade Bourbon label. The drink, like the horse, is stately and strong.

2 ounces Belle Meade Bourbon
¼ ounce maple syrup
1 dash Angostura bitters
1 dash Peychaud's bitters
Ice cubes
For serving: slice of orange peel

Add all ingredients to a mixing glass filled with ice. Stir briefly. Strain into a rocks glass over ice. Twist the orange peel over the drink and use it for garnish.

Texas foodways reflect the influence of Mexico to the immediate south, as well as foods brought in by Africans and by Europeans from Spain, Germany, and Czechoslovakia.

TEXAS

THE WIDE-OPEN SPACES OF TEXAS have made this state a comfortable home for cattle ranching. Not surprisingly, beef is the meat of choice. The Texas barbecue belt stretches across the heart of the state, serving up beef brisket and sausage, which is a modern extension of the state's German and Czech meat markets of the mid-nineteenth century.

Central Texas smokes meat for hours until it falls off the bone. West Texas beef barbecue has historically been cooked over direct heat using mesquite wood smoke. East Texas slow smokes meat over hickory, while South Texas likes a relatively sweet barbecue sauce.

Because Texas was once part of Mexico, it has a strong corn, squash, and bean tradition. The vast variety of native peppers that grow in Texas have given rise to a natural spice that has influenced cuisines around the world—ground, dried hot peppers. Over time, foods that developed from Mexican roots combined with non-Mexican sensibilities, creating the cuisine we know as Tex-Mex. This Americanized version of Mexican food has permeated the entire country, in both fast-food incarnations and in mom-and-pop restaurants. Salsa, the Tex-Mex sauce, for example, is now the most popular condiment in the United States. The corn-based chip Fritos has become mainstream American food, losing its connection to tortillas in the popular mind.

Despite some dissension, Texas is still southern. Foods such as mayhaw, sorghum, sugar, and the seafood of the Gulf Coast connect the state to the rest of the South. The Lone Star State is also partly southwestern, but we aren't going to cut Texas in half or forget that it is the crucible where those two borders interact.

LOW & SLOW SPICY BRISKET

MADDIE HAYES | MAKES 4 SERVINGS

This brisket is incredibly easy to make, with the oven doing all the work. The tender meat is perfect for tacos, enchiladas, on top of salads or po'boys, or in lasagna—you name it. If you're not a spice fiend like us, leave out the jalapeños. This recipe is wildly forgiving and customizable. Feel free to add different spices, herbs, chilis, citrus, vegetables, etc. Just have fun with it.

3–4 pounds beef brisket or chuck
1 large white onion, quartered
1–2 fresh jalapeño peppers, sliced lengthwise (optional)
8 ounces canned hatch green chiles, mild or spicy
Juice of an orange
Juice of 2 limes
2 bay leaves
1 cinnamon stick
Salt, to taste

Preheat the oven to 300°F. Place the brisket in a cast-iron Dutch oven or an oven-safe lidded pot. Add the onion, jalapeños, hatch green chiles, orange juice, and lime juice. Nestle in the bay leaves and cinnamon stick. Season with salt. Cover and bake at least 4 hours. Check every 30–60 minutes to make sure nothing is burning or sticking to the sides of the pot.

When ready, the brisket should be tender and falling apart. You should be able to shred it easily with a fork. At that point, turn the oven up to 425°F and take the lid off the pot. Bake until the liquid is reduced and the top of the meat is caramelized, about 1–2 hours. Don't overcook; the brisket should remain juicy and saucy.

CHILI

BRENDON BOTTOM | MAKES 4–6 SERVINGS

- 2 tablespoons olive oil
- 2 pounds ground beef
- 1 white onion, chopped
- 1 yellow bell pepper, chopped
- 5 cloves garlic, chopped
- 1 teaspoon salt
- 2 jalapeño peppers, chopped
- 2 serrano peppers, chopped
- 1 (8-ounce) can tomato sauce
- 2 tablespoons tomato paste
- 4 tablespoons chili powder
- 1 teaspoon ground cumin
- 1 teaspoon dried oregano
- 1 teaspoon cayenne pepper
- 2 (12-ounce) cans beer
- 1 (16-ounce) can kidney beans, drained and rinsed
- 1 (16-ounce) can pinto beans, drained and rinsed
- 1 (15-ounce) can petite diced tomatoes
- 1–2 cups beef stock or broth (optional)
- For serving: cheese, sour cream, cilantro, green onions, tortilla chips, etc.

Heat olive oil over medium-high heat in a large pot or Dutch oven. Add beef and break it up with the back of a wooden spoon. Cook until it is completely cooked through and is lightly crisp around the edges. Remove to a plate.

To the pot, add onion and bell pepper and sauté until translucent and starting to brown around the edges, about 7 minutes. Add garlic and salt, and cook until garlic is fragrant, 30 seconds. Add the jalapeños and serrano peppers. Reduce heat and add the tomato sauce, tomato paste, and all the herbs and spices. Deglaze the pan with the beer.

Stir in the kidney and pinto beans, the browned meat, and diced tomatoes. If you prefer your chili looser and saucier, add the stock. Cook low and slow, covered, at least 3 hours or up to 6. Garnish with cheese, sour cream, cilantro, green onions, tortilla chips, or whatever your heart desires. If it feels right to you, serve with cornbread, rolls, or biscuits. And we so choose.

SLOW COOKER CHARRO BEANS

STEPHANIE BOTTOM | MAKES 6 TO 8 SERVINGS

1 pound dried pinto beans
½ pound bacon
4 cups water
2 cups beef broth
6 cloves garlic, minced
1 fresh jalapeño pepper, diced
1 tablespoon powdered cumin
1 teaspoon garlic powder
1 teaspoon chili powder
1 (10-ounce) can Rotel-brand diced tomatoes and green chilis
1 cup coarsely chopped fresh cilantro leaves
Salt and pepper, to taste
For serving: hot cooked rice

Place the beans in a colander and rinse them well, removing stones and other debris. Cook the bacon by your favorite method until crisp. Drain, chop, and reserve.

Add the beans to a slow cooker, then stir in the bacon, water, broth, garlic, jalapeño, cumin, garlic powder, and chili powder. Cook on low 6 hours.

Stir in the Rotel tomatoes and then the cilantro leaves. Cook 1 more hour. Turn off the cooker and adjust for salt and pepper. Serve over rice or as a side dish.

COWBOY CAVIAR

MADDIE HAYES | MAKES 8 CUPS

Also known as Texas Caviar, this colorful, sharp, sweet side dish can also be served as an appetizer or a dip for tortilla chips. Cowboy Caviar was invented in the 1950s by Helen Corbitt, a New Yorker who ended up teaching cooking in Austin and later worked at the Dallas Neiman Marcus Zodiac Room; there she invented the original dish, which she called "pickled black-eyed peas."

¾ cup olive oil
¾ cup freshly squeezed lime juice
2–4 teaspoons honey
2 tablespoons powdered taco seasoning
Salt and ground black pepper, to taste
2 cups canned black beans or pinto beans, drained
2 cups canned black-eyed peas, drained
2 cups cooked corn
2 avocados, diced
1 large mango, cut into chunks (you can also use peaches)
1 medium red bell pepper, diced
1 medium orange bell pepper, diced
1 medium yellow bell pepper, diced
1 small to medium red onion, diced
½ cup sliced green onion
1–2 fresh jalapeño peppers, diced
Candied jalapeños (optional)
4–6 ounces cotija or feta cheese, crumbled

In a large bowl, mix olive oil, lime juice, honey, taco seasoning, salt, and black pepper. In the same bowl, add black beans, black-eyed peas, corn, avocados, mango, bell peppers, onion, green onion, fresh jalapeños, and optional candied jalapeños, Mix lightly together and add cheese. Combine thoroughly. Serve immediately or refrigerate several hours. It keeps in the refrigerator, covered, up to three days.

LINDA STALEY'S TEXAS CHOCOLATE SHEET CAKE

WYNNE HOBBS & HER GRANDMOTHER GIGI

MAKES 1 (18×13- OR 9×13-INCH) CAKE

This sheet cake is as big as Texas.

1 cup (2 sticks) butter
1 cup water
5 tablespoons cocoa powder
2 cups all-purpose flour
2 cups granulated sugar
1 teaspoon baking soda
½ teaspoon salt
½ cup buttermilk
2 large eggs
1 teaspoon vanilla extract
Chocolate Pecan Glaze (recipe follows)

Preheat the oven at 350°F. Grease and flour an 18×13-inch sheet pan or a 9×13-inch baking pan and set aside. In a saucepan set over medium-high heat, add butter, water, and cocoa, and bring to a boil. Into the saucepan, sift the flour, sugar, baking soda, and salt. Add buttermilk, eggs, and vanilla. Mix well and pour into the prepared pan.

Bake until the center springs back when lightly touched: 20 minutes for the sheet pan and 35–40 minutes for the 9×13-inch pan. Five minutes before the cake is completely baked, pull it out of the oven and pour over the glaze. Bake the remaining 5 minutes. Remove from the oven and cool.

CHOCOLATE PECAN GLAZE

½ cup (1 stick) butter
6 tablespoons buttermilk
5 tablespoons cocoa powder
1 (1-pound) box confectioners' sugar, sifted
1 teaspoon vanilla extract
1 cup chopped pecans

In a large saucepan set over medium heat, melt together the butter, buttermilk, and cocoa. Cook long enough to completely melt the butter. Remove from heat and stir in powdered sugar and vanilla. Stir in the pecans. Pour over the hot cake as directed.

OATMEAL CARMELITAS

STEPHANIE BOTTOM | MAKES 42 SQUARES

14 ounces Caramel Topping, cooled (recipe follows)
1½ cups, plus 4 tablespoons all-purpose flour
1½ cups quick cooking oats (not old-fashioned oatmeal)
1⅛ cups dark brown sugar
9 ounces (2 sticks, plus 2 tablespoons) unsalted butter, melted
¾ teaspoon baking soda
¼ cup salt
1½ cups semi-sweet chocolate chips
1½ cups chopped pecans

Preheat the oven to 350°F. Butter a 9×13-inch baking pan and set aside. Mix the caramel topping with the 4 tablespoons flour. Stir well and set aside.

In a large bowl, mix together the remaining 1½ cups flour, the oats, sugar, melted butter, baking soda, and salt. Press half the mixture into the prepared pan. Bake 10 minutes.

Remove from the oven and sprinkle with the chocolate chips. Pour the caramel mixture over the chocolate, followed by the pecans. Cover evenly with the rest of the oat mixture and press lightly to make a uniform thickness. Bake another 20 minutes. Remove from the oven and cool completely. If the chocolate is too runny, place in the refrigerator 1 hour. Cut into squares and store in an airtight container.

CARAMEL TOPPING

MAKES 14 OUNCES

1 (14-ounce) can sweetened condensed milk

Pour the entire can of condensed milk into a microwave-safe glass measuring cup or glass bowl. The glass cup or bowl should hold at least 2 quarts. Microwave on 50% power or medium (depending on your microwave) for 2 minutes.

Remove from the microwave and stir well. Cover the glass loosely with plastic wrap or another cover that will allow the steam to escape. Heat and stir every 2 minutes until the milk is the caramel color you like. This will take 10–14 minutes, depending on the power of your microwave. Use immediately over ice cream or allow it to cool to use in the recipe for Carmelitas.

SHOWER PUNCH

BRENT ROSEN | MAKES 19 (6-OUNCE) SERVINGS

When drinking in the shower, it's important to remember that water will get into your beverage. Whether that water comes from direct exposure to the spray from the shower, or through the accumulation of steam, or even from drops from the ceiling, water will get into your drink. That's no problem if you're drinking a Coors Light, but a big problem if you're drinking a cocktail that cannot take further dilution.

The solution? Mix a punch that's beer-based and full of spirit and flavor. That way, if water does make its way into your glass, it's a welcome guest. This punch tastes great but will hit rather hard. Add ice if you want to take the edge off and dilute it the old-fashioned way.

4 cups tequila blanco
3 cups lime juice
3 cups simple syrup
3 (12-ounce) cans cold beer
Dash of Tabasco sauce
Dash of Angostura bitters
Ice cubes (optional)

Mix all ingredients together in a large punch bowl. Feel no fear if you splash shower water in your glass while bathing.

MARGARITA

THE MUSEUM OF THE AMERICAN COCKTAIL

MAKES 1 COCKTAIL

While many people claim the margarita was invented in 1948 by Margarita Sames, there are many conflicting stories about its origins, some going back to the early 1930s. We take all stories with a pinch of salt. It is worth noting that Americans drank Tequila Daisies (liquor, orange liqueur, and citrus) as early as 1936 and Tequila Sidecars by 1944, while a 1937 British cocktail book included the Picador, made with 2 parts tequila to 1 part each Cointreau and lime juice.

1½ ounces tequila
1 ounce Cointreau
½ ounce lime juice
Ice cubes
Salt for rimming the glass

Shake the ingredients with ice. Strain into a salt-rimmed cocktail glass or into a salt-rimmed, ice-filled, margarita glass. If you salt only half the rim, then it works well both for people who like the salt rim and for those who don't.

Smoked ham is a dominant influence in defining the food of Virginia, but African Americans like Edna Lewis, featured here, took their personal food experiences and made the world appreciate the food of the South.

VIRGINIA

NATIVE AMERICANS IN EASTERN VIRGINIA thrived on corn, acorns, deer, bear, wild fowl, crabs, oysters, and fish. When English colonists arrived in the region, they had a difficult time surviving, despite the abundance of food. One reason is that European crops failed in the new environment. The Europeans turned to Native Americans for help, although early interactions with the Powhatan were not always peaceful. Eventually the colonists adopted corn, squash, and native tubers into their diet.

Regardless of what foods were available, the colonists continually tried to imitate and preserve the English style of eating. As the colonies became better established, the food served reflected the class structure of England, meaning that the upper classes dined in the French style. Most of the colonists, who were from the lower classes, ate one-pot dishes of mush or salted meat. There was a universal practice of preserving foods for the colder months when crops could not be grown. Thus, meats were salted and smoked, vegetables were pickled, and fruits were dried and canned.

Enslaved Africans ate meagerly, even as they prepared multicourse meals for the white middle and upper classes. As in other southern states, African slaves brought many native foods to Virginia, including peas, peanuts, okra, and the technique of frying.

Today Virginia farmers commercially raise chickens, cattle, and turkeys. They grow corn, wheat, apples, and pumpkins. The state is rightly proud of its peanuts, as well as Smithfield hams. The Shenandoah Valley's Pennsylvania Dutch population is famous for scrapple, watermelon-rind pickles, and shoofly pie. Virginia certainly embraces modern culinary trends, but it proudly continues to hold on to its traditional foods.

DUKE'S PIMENTO CHEESE

BRENT ROSEN | MAKES 3 CUPS

Pimento cheese makes an appearance at most southern holiday gatherings. The savory spread is fun to make, fun to eat, and keeps in the refrigerator for days (if it lasts that long). This version uses roasted red peppers instead of the traditional pimento, which adds more flavor and punch. This recipe has the additional boost of southern-made Wickles Pickles Original Relish, which adds a spicy, sweet, and vinegary note that really cuts through the mayonnaise and cheese. The relish brings the whole dish together.

1 pound sharp yellow cheddar cheese
3 large red bell peppers, roasted (feel free to use jarred)
4 ounces cream cheese, softened
½ cup Duke's Mayonnaise
1 heaping tablespoon Wickles Original Relish (purchased from specialty stores or online)
1 teaspoon freshly ground black pepper
1 teaspoon sugar
⅛ teaspoon cayenne pepper (optional)
Splash of hot sauce, such as Tabasco or Tabasco sriracha

Grate the cheese with a box grater. (Packaged grated cheese has more moisture and will not combine with the other ingredients as well as freshly grated.) Transfer the cheese to a large bowl, and thoroughly blend in the remaining ingredients. Cover and refrigerate. Serve chilled. Keeps refrigerated up to 5 days.

VIRGINIA HAM SANDWICHES WITH NANA'S LIGHT ROLLS & SOUTHERN MAYONNAISE

AUBREY SEADER, HER MOTHER MELINDA SEADER & AUBREY'S NANA, MARYMARIE BRENEMAN HICKS

SERVES 24, BUT MAKE AS MANY AS YOU WANT

Virginia's early settlers salted and cured meats in the colder months. Early Jamestown settlers adapted the salt-curing and smoking methods of Native Americans, which differed from the traditional sun-dried English way.

In the winter, hams were packed with sea salt, hung to dry, hickory smoked for flavor, and allowed to age so that they could be eaten in the spring and summer. Today, hams are cured the same way at the Smithfield Packing Company, and Smithfield, the company's home city, has become known as the "Ham Capital of the World." The Smithfield Packing Company was founded in 1936 by Joseph W. Luter; the popularity of its ham has made it the largest producer of pork in the world.

Edwards Virginia Smokehouse of Surry also produces a popular Virginia ham. In 1926, S. Wallace Edwards began selling home-cured ham sandwiches on the Jamestown–Surry ferry. The demand was so great that he turned curing ham into a business. Today, Edwards Smokehouse continues to use Native American smoking and curing methods.

Nana's Light Rolls (recipe follows)
Southern Mayonnaise (recipe follows)
Sliced Virginia ham
Toppings of your choice

NANA'S LIGHT ROLLS

MAKES 24 ROLLS

2 packets yeast, dry or cake
½ cup, plus 1 tablespoon granulated sugar
1 cup warm water
4 cups bread flour, sifted
1 tablespoon salt
2 large eggs, beaten
⅓ cup shortening, melted

Dissolve the yeast and 1 tablespoon sugar in the warm water. In a large mixing bowl, sift together the ½ cup sugar, the flour, and the salt. Make a well in the center.

Add eggs and dissolved yeast. Then add shortening. Stir with a spoon until the dough is smooth. Grease the top of the dough, cover with a light damp cloth, and let sit in a warm place until it's doubled in size, about 1 hour. (If you don't have a "warm spot," put a few inches warm (not hot) water in your sink and sit the bowl in it.)

When the dough has doubled, grease a half-sheet baking pan. Flour a hard surface and knead the dough until smooth and pliable, about 15–20 minutes. Shape into 24 dough balls and arrange them on the prepared pan. (At this point you can put the rolls in the refrigerator. When ready to bake refrigerated dough, let rise at warm room temperature 2 hours before putting in the hot oven.) Cover with a light damp cloth, and let rise until doubled, about another hour. About 15 minutes before rolls have risen completely, preheat the oven to 350°F. Bake the rolls until lightly golden brown, about 25 minutes.

SOUTHERN MAYONNAISE

MAKES A SCANT PINT

1 large egg yolk
1 teaspoon Dijon mustard
1 cup neutral oil, like canola or peanut oil
1½ teaspoons freshly squeezed lemon juice
1 teaspoon grated lemon zest
½ teaspoon salt

Place the egg yolk and the mustard in a blender or small food processor. Puree on low speed. With the blender still running, add a few drops of oil. Add the rest of the oil in a thin stream. Mixture should be thick. Remove from the blender, and stir in the lemon juice, lemon zest, and salt. This mayonnaise lasts about 10 days in the refrigerator. It is not as thick as commercial mayonnaise, but it is delicious.

Assembly

To make sandwiches, slice the rolls lengthwise, and slather both sides with mayonnaise and any desired condiments. On one half of the roll, layer on the ham and any other sandwich fixings you have on hand. Top with the other half of the roll and serve.

SPICY PEANUT BUTTER SOUP

SERIGNE MBAYE | MAKES 6 SERVINGS

Virginia peanuts are one of four types of peanuts grown in America. They have a larger kernel than other peanuts and are typically roasted in the shell. It is said that the peanut arrived in Virginia in the 1600s and then spread to other colonies. Peanuts became a colonial Williamsburg and Virginia staple and have been enjoyed roasted or in soup. The Peanut Shop of Williamsburg is one of the state's most famous peanut roasters, and it prides itself on producing the finest Virginia peanuts.

Many grocers in the South sell raw peanuts in season. If you need them at other times, try a feed and seed store or the internet.

½ cup vegetable oil
1 medium white onion, chopped
1 cup raw, shelled green (freshly dug) peanuts
Salt
½ teaspoon white wine vinegar
1 small habanero pepper, diced (optional)
½ cup tomato paste
3 cups vegetable stock or water
1 cup peanut butter
Cayenne pepper
½–1 teaspoon brown sugar
For serving: cooked white or brown rice, 1 bunch chopped parsley, and ¼ cup roughly chopped roasted peanuts

In a saucepan over medium heat, heat the oil until it's hot and add the onion. (You want to hear a sizzle when you add the onion.) Sauté 2–3 minutes and then add the peanuts. Season with 1 teaspoon salt and stir frequently to ensure that the onions and peanuts don't burn. Once the peanuts and onions have softened and started to caramelize, deglaze the pan with vinegar. Add the habanero. (Remember, habaneros are extremely spicy.) Add the tomato paste and stir until the mixture turns a rusty, brick color. Tomato paste burns quickly, so don't walk away from the saucepan.

Pour in the vegetable stock. Simmer until saucy and glossy and the peanuts have softened, 10–20 minutes. Stir in the peanut butter and taste for salt. If you need more spice, add a dash of cayenne pepper. Stir in your preferred amount of brown sugar. Taste again for seasoning. If the soup seems too thick, add more vegetable stock.

Slowly pour the soup into a blender and puree until creamy. Serve hot in a bowl with rice. Top with parsley, chopped peanuts, and a dash of cayenne pepper.

MAC & CHEESE

STEPHANIE BOTTOM | MAKES 8 SERVINGS

This traditional recipe makes a great mac and cheese dish for kids.

1 pound macaroni, either elbow or a fun shape like farfalle
5 tablespoons butter, plus more for buttering the dish
4 tablespoons all-purpose flour
3 ½ cups whole milk
1 pound grated sharp cheddar cheese

Preheat the oven to 400°F. Butter a 2-quart oven-proof casserole dish and set aside. Cook macaroni according to package directions but for 4 minutes less than the suggested cooking time. Remove from heat, drain, and set aside.

In a saucepan over medium heat, stir the 5 tablespoons butter and the flour together until the butter is completely melted. Cook and stir until the flour no longer tastes raw, about 2 minutes. Add the milk and continue stirring until the milk begins to bubble around the edges of the pot. As the liquid begins to thicken, add the cheese and continue stirring until the cheese is melted. Add the macaroni and stir well. Pour into the prepared dish and bake until it bubbles around the sides, 20 minutes. Serve warm.

BUTTERMILK CHESS PIE

MADDIE HAYES | MAKES 1 (9-INCH) PIE

Chess pie is a popular dessert in Virginia and is nothing more than a single pie crust filled with a mixture of eggs, butter, flour, and sugar. Some recipe variations add cornmeal instead of flour and different flavorings, such as vanilla, lemon, coconut, or chocolate. The origin of the name "chess pie" is uncertain. Some believe that the name came from the way "it's just pie" sounds with a southern accent: "it's jes' pie." Others suggest that the pie was named after the term "pie safe" (a cupboard or chest for pie). Yet others suggest that the name could have been derived from the term "cheese pie," which refers to traditional English lemon curd pie.

1 (9-inch) unbaked homemade or store-bought pie crust
1½ cups granulated sugar
½ cup (1 stick) salted butter, melted
⅓ cup buttermilk
2 tablespoons fine cornmeal
1 tablespoon all-purpose flour
1 tablespoon lemon juice
1 tablespoon finely grated lemon zest
1 teaspoon vanilla extract
¼ teaspoon salt
4 large eggs
For serving: confectioners' sugar or whipped cream (optional)

Preheat the oven to 425°F. Line the unbaked pie crust with aluminum foil. Fill with dried beans or pie weights and bake 5 minutes. (This weighted baking technique is called "blind baking.") Remove the weights and foil. Bake until golden and lightly fragrant, about 5 more minutes. Cool completely.

In a bowl, thoroughly combine sugar, butter, buttermilk, cornmeal, flour, lemon juice, lemon zest, and vanilla. Add the eggs and salt and mix well. Pour the mixture into the cooled pie crust.

Turn the oven temperature down to 350°F and bake 10 minutes. Place aluminum foil around the edges to prevent burning. Bake until the center is set, 40–55 more minutes. Transfer to a wire rack and cool 30 minutes. When ready to serve, dust with confectioners' sugar or top with a dollop of whipped cream. Store pie in the refrigerator.

HEAVENLY HASH

DAVID GUAS | MAKES ABOUT 6 SMALL PIECES OF CANDY

David Guas's Bayou Bakery, Coffee Bar and Eatery in Arlington, Virginia, is famous for this confection, which is a favorite throughout the South.

1 cup granulated sugar
1 cup evaporated milk
2 tablespoons light corn syrup
12 ounces semi-sweet chocolate, chopped or chips
1 teaspoon vanilla extract
½ teaspoon salt
2 cups pecan pieces, toasted and cooled to room temperature
2 cups mini-marshmallows

Lightly grease a 9 × 11-inch pan. Combine sugar, milk, and corn syrup in a 4-quart saucepan. Bring to a boil over medium heat, stirring constantly, and then cook for exactly 2½ minutes. Remove from heat and whisk in chocolate, vanilla, and salt. Cool slightly, about 15 minutes.

Stir in pecans and marshmallows. Pour mixture onto the prepared pan. Wrap in plastic wrap and refrigerate at least 4 hours or overnight. Cut into 1–1½ inch squares. Serve chilled or at room temperature.

Photo courtesy of David Guas.

MADEIRA COBBLER

THE MUSEUM OF THE AMERICAN COCKTAIL | MAKES 1 COCKTAIL

A venerable American beverage especially popular in the nineteenth century, the cobbler probably got its name from the "cobbles" of ice it contained. Traditionally, this drink is a simple mixture of wine (preferably sherry), sugar, and ice, shaken with a couple of orange slices and served with a straw.

2 (1-inch) wedges fresh pineapple (one without skin, one with)
2 slices orange
2 slices lemon
¾ ounce raspberry syrup or raspberry liqueur
1 ounce water
Crushed ice
2 ounces madeira wine

In a mixing glass, muddle the pineapple wedge without skin, 1 orange slice, 1 lemon slice, the raspberry syrup, and 1 ounce water. Add ice and the madeira and shake well. Strain into a double old-fashioned glass filled with crushed ice. Garnish with an orange slice, the remaining pineapple wedge, and a lemon slice.

MULLED WINE

BRENT ROSEN | MAKES 8 (4-OUNCE) SERVINGS

Mulled wine is a holiday classic, but it's tasty all year round. This mulled wine is delicious, but you're not making this large-format cocktail only for its flavor: mulled wine will fill your house with scents of cinnamon, clove, anise, and citrus. You are basically making potpourri that you can drink with friends and family. Satsuma and cane syrup are strong flavors: use a big and bold red wine like a cabernet or a zinfandel so that the taste of the wine doesn't get shouldered out of the picture.

4 cups apple cider
1 (750-ml) bottle of bold red wine
¼ cup cane syrup
2 cinnamon sticks
10 kumquats, halved
Zest and juice of two large satsumas or oranges
4 whole cloves
3 star anise
For garnish: orange peel

In a large saucepan, combine the cider, wine, cane syrup, cinnamon sticks, kumquats, satsuma zest and juice, cloves, and star anise. Bring to a boil and simmer over low heat for 10 minutes. Strain into mugs. Add an orange peel to each mug and serve.

Manufactured goods are a part of the West Virginia economy, including colorful Fiesta dinnerware. The state is known for such diverse delicacies as pizza rolls and pickled ramps.

WEST VIRGINIA

AS IN THE REST OF THE SOUTH, the food of West Virginia is shaped by geography. The state's mountainous terrain limits its agricultural space and historically made the region more isolated than other parts of the South. Minimal migrations resulted in less trade and even less introduction of diverse foods and cuisines.

Because of West Virginia's historical isolation, salt and pepper are the traditional seasonings. In the days before modern transportation, as well as in times of scarcity, cooks often made pepper from dried and ground buds of the native spicebush shrub. It was also common to forage, with foods like dandelion greens and wild apples appearing often on tables.

The traditional dishes of West Virginia are simple fare: chicken pie, wild game such as hares and squirrel, biscuits, and sausage gravy. Fried chicken is a noted specialty. Other favorites include beans, fried green tomatoes, pork, chicken, and cured meats. West Virginians also enjoy eating native crawfish, called crawdads, and fish, as well as local honey and sorghum.

West Virginia's state food is the pepperoni roll, a bread roll filled with a stick of pepperoni. It was invented by an Italian immigrant as a portable and convenient lunch for coal miners.

The Golden Delicious variety of apple was first grown as a chance seedling tree on the Mullins's family farm in Clay County in the early 1900s. Thousands of acres in West Virginia are planted in apples, as well as peaches. Buckwheat pancakes are popular for breakfast, and there are buckwheat festivals around the state. Each year festivals and public dinners also celebrate wild mountain leeks, known as ramps. The annual Cast Iron Cook Off honors the state's cooking traditions.

As in many southern states, West Virginia has a movement to save and preserve heritage vegetable seeds. Many of these heirloom seeds come from older farmers who have grown crops from seeds their families have planted for decades.

Photo courtesy of Steve McHugh.

CHOW-CHOW

STEVE MCHUGH* | MAKES 2 QUARTS

This southern relish staple is often canned during the harvest season and provides vegetables during the lean winter months. It is so versatile that it enhances the flavor of almost any savory dish.

3 cups water
2½ teaspoons salt
2 teaspoons sugar
4 cloves garlic, smashed
1 jalapeño pepper, cut in half
2 bay leaves
1 tablespoon coriander seeds
1 tablespoon dill seeds
1 cup medium-diced onion
1 pound zucchini, medium dice
1 pound corn kernels
1 cup climbing beans, cooked (any bean or pea can be substituted, such as black-eyed peas, purple hull peas, romano beans, black beans, etc.)

To make the brine, mix the water, salt, and sugar in a pot set over medium-high heat, and simmer until sugar is dissolved. Cool to room temperature.

In a 2-quart crock or glass container, place the garlic, jalapeño, bay leaves, coriander, and dill. In a separate bowl, mix the onion, zucchini, corn, and beans, and add the mixture to the crock. Cover with the room-temperature brine and seal airtight. Ferment at room temperature 3–14 days. Taste the chow-chow daily, beginning at day 3. When the taste is right, store in the refrigerator.

CHICKEN-FRIED STEAK & GRAVY

MADDIE HAYES | MAKES 4 SERVINGS

CHICKEN-FRIED STEAK

4 thin beef ribeye steaks
1 cup all-purpose flour
2 teaspoons seasoned salt
¾ teaspoon paprika
¼ teaspoon cayenne pepper
Salt and freshly ground black pepper
3 large eggs
½ cup milk
2 cups unseasoned breadcrumbs
2 cups neutral frying oil, like canola or peanut oil
For serving: lemon wedges

To make the steak, use a meat hammer, a skillet, a rolling pin, or even an empty wine bottle to pound the ribeye thin, about ½–¼ inch. Set up an assembly line for breading. In the first bowl, whisk together the flour, seasoned salt, paprika, cayenne, salt, and black pepper. In another bowl, whisk together the eggs and milk. Put the breadcrumbs in a third bowl.

Season the ribeye with salt and pepper and dredge in the seasoned flour. Shake off any excess flour. Dip the meat in the milk and egg mixture. Dredge the ribeye in the breadcrumbs and toss lightly to coat evenly.

Heat the oil in a large cast-iron skillet over medium heat to 365°F. Fry each ribeye separately until browned, roughly 3–5 minutes on each side. Make sure the oil doesn't get too hot—it should not be smoking at any point. Remove the steak from the oil, and place on a paper-towel-lined plate. If needed, add more oil to the pan. Make sure to bring the oil back up to the correct temperature before repeating process with the remaining steaks.

GRAVY

2 tablespoons salted butter or pan drippings
2 tablespoons all-purpose flour
1 cup homemade or store-bought chicken stock
½ cup whole milk
2 tablespoons lemon juice
Salt and freshly ground black pepper, to taste
Juice of 1 lemon

As the steaks cook, make the gravy. In a saucepan, melt the butter over medium heat. Stir in the flour and cook until the mixture is light golden brown, about 4 minutes, all the while whisking constantly and diligently scraping up the browned bits of flour. Gradually stir in the chicken stock and then the milk. Bring to a boil while whisking constantly, and cook until the gravy thickens, about 5 minutes. Add the lemon juice, and season with salt and pepper. If too thick, add more stock.

To serve, pour gravy over each chicken-fried steak and top with a lemon wedge.

PEPPERONI ROLLS

DANIEL SCHUMACHER | MAKES 12 ROLLS

The pepperoni roll was first sold commercially in 1927 by Giuseppe "Joseph" Argiro at the Country Club Bakery in Fairmont. The sandwich is still sold in bakeries and convenience stores throughout West Virginia as a classic lunch. It's arguably the most iconic food of West Virginia.

The traditional pepperoni roll is a soft yeast roll baked with a stick of pepperoni in the middle. When baked, the pepperoni fat melts and absorbs into the bread. Because it is easily portable, the roll was a popular lunch item among Italian immigrant coal miners of the early twentieth century.

Cooking spray
12 (1¼-ounce) pieces frozen yeast dinner roll dough
8–12 ounces pepperoni, thinly sliced
¾ cup shredded low-moisture whole-milk mozzarella cheese
1 large egg white
1 teaspoon water
Flaked sea salt (optional)

Preheat the oven to 350°F. Spray a baking sheet with cooking spray and place dough pieces 2 inches apart. Spray dough with cooking spray and cover with plastic wrap. Let stand at room temperature until thawed and doubled in size, about 4 hours.

Spray a hard work surface with cooking spray. Gently stretch each risen dough piece to about a 3 × 5-inch rectangle. Lay dough pieces horizontally and place 4 slices of pepperoni down each center. Top the pepperoni with 1 tablespoon cheese. Stretch the dough around the fillings and pinch to seal. Place rolls seam-side down on the baking sheet. Cover with plastic wrap and let rest at room temperature for 30 minutes.

In a small bowl, whisk together egg white and water, and brush the mixture on the dough pieces. If desired, top with a sprinkle of flaked sea salt. Bake until golden brown, 15 to 20 minutes. Serve warm or at room temperature.

QUICK PICKLED RAMPS

ELIZABETH M. WILLIAMS | MAKES 1 PINT

Ramps (*Allium tricoccum*) are a wild onion that grows in eastern Canada and the United States. Also called wild leeks, this springtime treat has light green leaves and a white bulb, and both parts are edible. Ramps have an oniony garlic flavor and have long been a staple of Cherokee and Appalachian cuisine and medicine. They are frequently fried, baked into cornbread, pickled, or used to replace onions and garlic. The Feast of the Ramson is a ramp festival hosted in Richwood, and the Ramps and Rails Festival takes place in Elkins.

1 cup water
1 cup apple cider vinegar
2 cloves garlic
1 bay leaf, cut into two
1 tablespoon whole coriander
1 tablespoon coarsely cracked black pepper
2 teaspoons sugar
1 teaspoon salt
2 cups trimmed, washed ramps, from 1–2 bunches fresh ramps, with stringy roots and green tops removed

Place all the ingredients except the ramps into a saucepan and bring to a boil. Boil 1 minute. Meanwhile, pack the ramps, bulb side down, into two clean ½-pint glass canning jars. Remove the boiling brine from the heat. Use a spoon to divide the spices between the two jars, making sure to put one clove and a piece of bay leaf in each. Ladle in the brine, being sure it covers the ramps. Cap the jars and refrigerate 48 hours. Store in the refrigerator up to 2 weeks.

NANA'S SQUASH CASSEROLE

BETH WITHERSPOON HAYES | MAKES 4 TO 6 SERVINGS

Butter for greasing the pan
6–8 medium yellow squash, sliced
1 large Vidalia onion, roughly chopped
1 clove garlic, chopped
Salt and pepper, to taste
2 cups grated sharp cheddar cheese, divided
1 stack of Ritz crackers, crushed, divided
1 large egg, at room temperature, beaten
¼ cup milk, if needed

Preheat the oven to 400°F. Butter a 2-quart glass casserole dish and set aside. Place the squash, onion, garlic, salt, and pepper in a pot. Cover the ingredients with water and bring to a boil. Reduce heat to low and cook until tender, 20–30 minutes. Drain the squash mixture well and mash with a fork or potato masher. Place the vegetables in a mixing bowl and let cool.

Add 1 cup cheese, 1¼ cups of the crushed crackers, and the beaten egg. Mix with a spoon. If the mixture seems dry, add a little milk, but you don't want it too soupy. Pour into the buttered casserole dish and bake until you see a little browning around the edges, 25 minutes or so. Sprinkle on the remaining crushed Ritz crackers and then cover with the remaining cup of cheese. Return the casserole to the oven and bake until the cheese is completely melted, about 5 minutes. Serve warm.

MINI APPLE PIES

JENNIE MERRILL BOUDREAUX | MAKES 12

3 unbaked (9-inch) rounds of pie dough
5 medium tart apples, peeled and chopped
¾ cup granulated sugar
4 tablespoons all-purpose flour
1 tablespoon freshly squeezed lemon juice
1 teaspoon cinnamon
¼ teaspoon nutmeg
2 tablespoons chilled butter

Preheat the oven to 425°F. Roll the pie dough ¼–⅛ inch thick. Cut out twelve 4-inch rounds of dough from the pie crusts and reserve any scraps. Press each dough circle down into a mini-muffin tin, allowing the top edges of the crust to run up and out the sides.

In a bowl, mix the apples, sugar, flour, lemon juice, cinnamon, and nutmeg. Let sit 10 minutes. Cut the butter into 12 pieces. Spoon the apple mixture into the crusts and add 1 piece of butter in each cup. Use any remaining dough scraps to decorate the tops of the pies. Bake until the crust is light brown and the apples are bubbling, 16–18 minutes. Serve warm.

SWEET TEA

ELIZABETH M. WILLIAMS | MAKES 2 QUARTS

No cookbook about the South would be complete without a mention of sweet tea. Although south Louisiana is an outlier in not meaning sweet tea when saying "iced tea," almost the entire South considers unsweetened tea to be unfinished. The best compromise for those times that you need both sweet tea and unsweetened tea is to make unsweetened tea and serve it next to a bottle of simple syrup for sweet tea drinkers to use. That way they won't have undissolved sugar in the bottom of their glasses.

2 quarts water
1 cup granulated sugar, or more or less depending on how sweet you like it
3 tablespoons loose-leaf orange pekoe tea, in a tea ball
For serving: ice cubes, fresh mint, and lemon wedges

Boil the water and stir in the sugar. When the sugar has dissolved, remove from the heat, and add the tea ball of tea. Steep 20 minutes or until the tea reaches your desired strength.

Remove the tea ball, pour the brewed tea into a pitcher, and refrigerate it until cool. When chilled, serve over ice in a tall glass garnished with a sprig of mint and a lemon wedge.

APPALACHIAN PUNCH

BRENT ROSEN | MAKES 10 SERVINGS

4 each, lemons, oranges, and limes
3 cups sparkling wine, chilled
2 cups moonshine, chilled
2 cups seltzer, chilled
1¼ cups granulated sugar
For serving: shaved ice and lemon, orange, and lime twists

Thinly slice lemons, oranges, and limes and layer them on the bottom of a punch bowl. Pour in the sparkling wine, moonshine, seltzer, and sugar and stir until sugar dissolves.

Fill classic punch glasses with shaved ice and punch. Garnish with triple bouquets of lemon, orange, and lime twists.

ACKNOWLEDGMENTS

SO MANY WONDERFUL AND GENEROUS PEOPLE have contributed to this book. We called on dear friends and relatives for recipes and inspiration. They read and edited copy and were terrific sounding boards for ideas and directions.

The members of the SoFAB family—staff, former staff, and interns, including our terrific volunteers—have been invaluable in sharing their memories, sifting through ideas and photos, and helping decide what is most important to share about SoFAB.

The SoFAB Board has been most supportive with kind words, recipes, and other help in crafting our story.

A big thank you to Alisa Plant, director of LSU Press, for having the vision to see that this book will be the takeaway from a visit to the museum for a long time into the future. And a special thanks to our editor, Cynthia Nobles, for being so patient, thoughtful, and helpful. She makes everything we've written so much better. We've been so fortunate to have our incredible team at LSU Press; they've worked so diligently to make this book into what we hope will be a family favorite. We can't thank them enough!

RECIPE CONTRIBUTORS

COLLEEN ALLERTON-HOLLIER is a chef, caterer, educator, and New Orleans native living in New York City.

LAURA BELLUCCI is a master cocktail maker and drinks consultant.

CHRISTOPHER BLAKE was a chef and cookbook writer, once called the "gourmet laureate of New Orleans" by Mayor Ernest "Dutch" Morial.

BRIGITTE BLEDSOE is the corporate executive chef of Miss Shirley Café in Baltimore.

BRENDON BOTTOM is a native of Corpus Christi, Texas, who is now living in New Orleans.

STEPHANIE BOTTOM, of Corpus Christi, Texas, is a retired elementary school principal and an enthusiastic cook and baker.

JENNIE MERRILL BOUDREAUX is the former director of education at SoFAB.

BYRON BRADLEY is the chef and co-owner of 2Brothers1Love, a catering company in New Orleans.

DICKIE BRENNAN is the owner of Brennan's Restaurant and several other restaurants in New Orleans.

GINA CHERSEVANI is the founder and owner of Buffalo & Bergen, a cocktail and bagel shop in Washington, DC.

NINA COMPTON is the chef/owner of Compère Lapin, the James Beard Foundation Award–winning restaurant in New Orleans, and a national TV personality.

JAMES CRUSE was the chef and pitmaster at Central City Barbecue in New Orleans.

CASSIDEE DABNEY is the chef at Blackberry Farm in Walland, Tennessee.

DAVID GUAS is the chef/owner of Bayou Bakery in Arlington, Virginia.

BETH WITHERSPOON HAYES is a real estate broker in Little River, South Carolina.

MADDIE HAYES, formerly the programs and curatorial manager at SoFAB, is a Charleston, South Carolina, native living and cooking in New Orleans, having returned from Anna Tasca Lanza Cooking School in Sicily.

MIKIE HAYES is an Atlanta, Georgia, native now living in Charleston, South Carolina.

VINCE HAYWARD is the fourth-generation owner and CEO of Camellia Brand beans in Elmwood, Louisiana.

JAMES HENSLEY is the operations manager of Nelson's Green Brier Distillery, in Nashville.

WYNNE HOBBS is a physician assistant born and bred in Dallas, Texas.

WAYNE JACOB is the owner of a historic smokehouse and restaurant in Laplace, Louisiana.

JULIA JOHNSTON is a Florida food maven and member of the SoFAB Board of Directors.

MATT KONIGSMARK lives in Georgia and was a cofounder of SoFAB.

DEE LAVIGNE operates a cooking school at SoFAB.

SERIGNE MBAYE is a Senegalese chef with Dakar Nola, a restaurant in New Orleans.

ASHBELL MCELVEEN is the founder of the James Hemings Society.

STEVE MCHUGH is the chef/owner of Cured in San Antonio.

CHUCK PURVIS worked for A. C. Legg, which has made seasonings for home and commercial use since 1923 in Calera, Alabama.

BRINLEY RHYS is an Atlanta native now living in New Orleans.

BRENT ROSEN is the former president and CEO of the Southern Food & Beverage Museum.

DANIEL SCHUMACHER is the former editor of *Louisiana Cookin'* magazine. He now lives in West Virginia.

AUBREY SEADER is an arts and health researcher in Bloomington, Indiana.

CAMILLE STAUB is a chef, caterer, and educator in New Orleans and the director of operations at SoFAB.

POPPY TOOKER, a native New Orleanian, is a cookbook author and host of the WWNO radio show *Louisiana Eats.*

ELIZABETH M. WILLIAMS is the founder and former president of the National Food and Beverage Foundation, which includes the Southern Food & Beverage Museum among its divisions.

TRES WILSON is an Alabama native and chef.

ASHLEY ROSE YOUNG was the first summer intern (2009) and guest curator (2011–2012) at the Southern Food & Beverage Museum. She now works at the Smithsonian Museum.

GENERAL INDEX

M

N

T

RECIPE INDEX

A

B

C

T